Lenten Studies, Sermons,
and Worship Resources
for Ash Wednesday
to Easter

GLORY IN THE CROSS

FRUIT OF THE SPIRIT FROM THE PASSION OF CHRIST

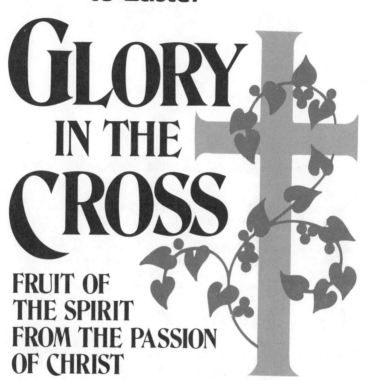

Gerhard Aho
Kenneth Rogahn
Richard Kapfer

CONCORDIA®

Publishing House
St. Louis

Library of Congress Cataloging in Publication Data

Aho, Gerhard.
    Glory in the cross—fruit of the Spirit from the passion of Christ.

    1. Lenten sermons. 2. Bible. N.T. Galatians V, 22-2—Sermons.
3. Lutheran Church—Sermons. 4. Sermons, American. 5. Lent—Prayer-books and devotions—English. I. Rogahn, Kenneth, 1936- . II. Kapfer, Richard G. III. Title.
BV4277.A38 1984   252'.62   84-7045
ISBN 0-570-03940-1

1 2 3 4 5 6 7 8 9 10   PP   93 92 91 90 89 88 87 86 85 84

"The fruit
of the Spirit is
love, joy,
peace, patience,
kindness, goodness,
faithfulness, gentleness,
self-control."

Gal. 5:22-23a (RSV)

Contents

Preface

In Galatians Paul presents his famous Magna Charta of the Church. In it he expresses the profound thought that "for freedom Christ has set us free." The topic of Christian freedom occupied Paul's attention in this epistle because of his concern over attempts to pervert this great freedom. Christian freedom should not provide opportunity for lawlessness, nor should it be replaced by bondage to another law. For Paul his freedom in Christ meant true freedom: freedom through love to be servants of one another. Such freedom does not glory in works of the flesh; "far be it from me to glory," Paul says, "except in the cross of our Lord Jesus Christ." We, like Paul, "glory in the cross" as we walk by the Spirit and show forth the fruit of the Spirit in our lives.

Glory in the Cross — Fruit of the Spirit from the Passion of Christ is a Lenten worship resource focusing on the fruit of the Spirit manifested by Christ in His Passion. Its goal is to encourage this fruit in the lives of believers. It is designed to assist Lenten worship preparation in several ways. Sermonic studies including three sermon outlines for each service are provided to assist individual sermon preparation. Fully prepared sermons for each service are provided for those who, in the press of pastoral responsibilities, are looking for developed resources. Sample liturgies which support the theme of the day are included for each service.

The idea for this series originally came from a pre-Lenten retreat sponsored by the Board for Evangelism Services under the direction of Dr. Erwin Kolb. Special thanks is extended to him for his assistance on this project. Concordia Publishing House extends limited permission to churches to duplicate the liturgies for congregational use.

The Publisher

Part I:
Sermonic Studies
by Gerhard Aho

Gentleness in Light of John 13:3-5 (1-17)

Comment on "Fruit of the Spirit"

"Fruit" in Gal. 5:22 is juxtaposed to "works" in verse 19. The term *fruit* denotes qualities or states of mind, habits of feeling, more than concrete actions. *Fruit* is often used in the New Testament to describe a product that is both pleasant and useful. In Luke 3:8 John the Baptist asks his hearers to "bear fruits that befit repentance." In John 15:2-16 Jesus speaks about fruit that will be produced by those who are attached to Him, the true Vine. In John 12:24 there is a reference to fruit borne by wheat. The fruit of righteousness is referred to in Phil. 1:11 and Heb. 12:11. Fruit gathered by the evangelist is spoken of in John 4:36 and in Rom. 1:13.

The genitive case in Gal. 5:22 denotes that these fruits belong to the Spirit in the sense that the Spirit influences Christians to produce them. The one producing the fruits is the Christian, but the Christian is acting under the influence of the Holy Spirit. The fruits do not therefore appear without strenuous endeavor on the part of the Christian. Nevertheless, because they are fruits of the Spirit, every Christian has them to a greater or a lesser degree. The reason Paul lists the fruits here is to prompt Christians to produce these fruits more fully by the operation of the Spirit within them. It is significant too that Paul uses the singular "fruit" rather than "fruits." The singular emphasizes that the fruits make up an organic unity. They are consistent with each other. One fruit does not take away from another. If a Christian has more of one fruit, he will not necessarily have less of another. "Fruit" points to wholeness and harmony. That is not the case with the works of the flesh described in verses 19-21. These works are confusing and conflicting, one contending with the other for mastery in a human being.

Finally, that these are fruits of the Spirit reminds us that they do not come only by practice or habit, nor will they be displayed if a person is simply instructed in them. Rather, it is essential for our spirit to be possessed by the Holy Spirit. There must be an inner change. The fruit grows from within. A bad tree cannot produce good fruit. At the same time, the good tree must be pruned and its fruit protected from frost and insects. The development of the fruit must be watched all along.

Word Study of Gentleness*

Usage in secular Greek. The word *praus* is etymologically related to *friend,* denoting that which is pleasant and gentle in opposition to roughness, bad temper, sudden anger, and brusqueness. Thus *praus* meant a mild and gentle friendliness. Among the Greeks gentle friendliness was highly prized as a social virtue. But it needed to be compensated so as not to be a fault. It should not lead to self-abasement.

Old Testament usage. The closest Hebrew term for gentleness is *āni.* In Num. 12:3 Moses is described as a very meek or humble man, and Ps. 76:9 speaks of the humble of the earth. *Ani* is a social and economic term referring to a person in the position of a servant who has no property and who must therefore serve others. In later usage, however, it takes on the sense of humble, referring to a person who is subject, who feels himself to be in a servant relationship to God, and who subjects himself to God quietly and without resistance. Perhaps the reason the Hebrew word is translated *prauteis* in the LXX is that this Greek term often had the sense of calm acceptance of fate or of human injustice.

Developments in the period of the prophets caused the word to take on additional meaning. The prophets in the early period castigated the sins of the wealthy. In the lowly, the poor of the land (Job 24:4), there developed the sense of being the bearers of the divine promise (Ps. 37:11). Despite outward lowliness, there was consciousness of divine good pleasure (Joel 3:10). An aspect of this divine good pleasure was God's deliverance of the lowly in the future glorious day, as in Job 36:15 where we are told that God delivers the afflicted. Quiet, patient, hopeful waiting without resistance (Ps. 37:9), complaint, or vehement anger was regarded as a sign of piety.

New Testament usage. In Matt. 11:28-30 Jesus speaks of Himself as meek or gentle. Jesus exemplified this gentleness abundantly with the woman at Jacob's well (John 4:7-26), with the father of the boy possessed by a demon (Mark 9:17-27), with a disciple about to betray Him (Luke 22:47-48), with another disciple who doubted His resurrection (John 20:26-29), and with those who nailed Him to the cross (Luke 23:34). He showed gentleness also when He rode into Jerusalem on Palm Sunday in fulfillment of the prophecy of Zech. 9:9. Jesus, as the fulfillment of the prophecy, is depicted as nonviolent and nonwarlike and thus radically opposed to people like the Zealots. In Matt. 5:5 Jesus includes the gentle among those who are blessed. Only Matthew of the Synoptists uses *praus,* and in these three passages: Matt. 5:5; 11:29; 21:5.

Other New Testament passages in which *praus* is used are the following. In 2 Cor. 10:1, although Paul has been inveighing against the Corinthians' disputatiousness and arrogance, he can still bring the gentleness of Christ to bear upon them. This gentleness has its basis in agape. The fact that Paul's gentleness rested on the love of Christ points up the essential difference between

---

*For many of the insights in this and in all eight succeeding word studies, I am indebted to essays in *Theological Dictionary of the New Testament,* 10 vol., ed. Gerhard Kittel and trans. Geoffrey W. Bromiley (Grand Rapids: Wm B. Eerdmans, 1964).

the fruits of the Spirit listed in Gal. 5 and pagan virtues. To have these fruits is to put on Christ. To produce them is to experience the operation of the Spirit of the indwelling Christ.

Another insight into gentleness is given in Gal. 6:1, where it is made clear that gentleness enables the Christian to correct an erring brother without arrogance, impatience, or anger. In Col. 3:12 gentleness is one of the gifts of election, and in Eph. 4:2 it is one of the gifts of "the calling to which you have been called" (4:1).

In 2 Tim. 2:25 the servant of Christ is to exercise gentleness in the correction of the lawless, in this way perhaps to snatch them away from Satan. In Titus 3:2 gentleness is commanded in relation to all. In 1 Peter 3:16, when authorities ask for an account of the Christian life of faith, it is to be given with meekness, even though the injustice that has been suffered might cause indignation or defiance. James 1:21 refers to meek readiness to be taught by the Word without flaring up at the teacher. In James 3:13 the righteous demonstrate gentleness in their whole walk, and this is in pleasing contrast to bitter zeal and contentiousness (3:14).

Text Study of John 13:3-5 (1-17)

General setting of text. John supplements the synoptic narrative by supplying information about Christ's first year of public ministry. The Synoptists give mainly the Galilean, Perean, and Judaean ministry, while John adds considerable material from the Jerusalem ministry.

John's gospel sets forth a view of Christ that stresses His deity and saving work. The purpose is stated in John 20:30.

Immediate context. The preceding verse (v. 2) refers to the devil having put into the heart of Judas to betray Christ. The connection with the opening verse of the text is that Jesus knew this, as well as the power that had been put into His hands by the Father. Even in the betrayal God was in control, for Christ's deliverance into the hands of His enemies would be a means whereby He would return to the Father from whom He had come. In the following verse (v. 6) Peter remonstrates, "Lord, do You wash my feet?" The thought unit in verses 6-9 is Jesus' explanation to Peter of why He must wash Peter's feet. The thought unit in verses 1-2 is Jesus' awareness of His approaching departure from the world.

In verses 10-11 the washing of the feet symbolizes spiritual cleansing. Only John records the episode of the footwashing. The words recorded by Luke in 22:25-30 (amplified by John), in which Jesus speaks to the disciples about humility, seem to have followed upon the foot-washing episode.

It is significant that Jesus performs this service to His disciples even though He knew of the resolution that had ripened in Judas and even though He was fully aware that all things had been put into His hands and that He was at the threshold of glory. He washed even Judas's feet.

Text in vernacular. There are no significant variations in the English translations.

Text in original. V.3. The Greek word *eidōs* is placed first for emphasis to accent the full consciousness of Jesus regarding His deity. The verbs for "rise" and "lay aside" are in the dramatic present. V. 4. The *himatia* is the outer robe, so that now Jesus had only His tunic on as One who served.

Doctrinal study. Peter's reaction was natural in view of his awareness of who he was and who Jesus was. Jesus, however, explains that the washing is a token of the spiritual cleansing the disciples needed from daily sins.

But this rite is also a symbol of mutual service and helpfulness—not that we literally wash one another's feet, but that we "bear one another's burdens, and so fulfil the law of Christ" (Gal. 6:2). The lowliness and gentleness of Christ are far removed from the vain glory displayed by the disciples who argued about who was the greatest. True greatness is gauged by self-denying service.

Parallel passages. Matt. 20:20-28 and Mark 10:35-45 (the request of James and John for seats of honor at Christ's right and left hand) are important for the background of the text. Other key passages are Matt. 5:44; Luke 6:29; 12:37; Rom. 12:14, 17, 19, 20, 21; and 1 Peter 5:5.

Central thought. By washing His disciples' feet, Jesus gives us an example of gentleness in service.

Homiletical Treatment

Goal-malady-means approach. The goal is that the hearers will more fully demonstrate Christ's gentleness. The malady is that we sometimes regard gentleness as a sign of weakness and cowardly submissiveness. The Gospel means to achieve the goal is that Jesus by His death secured for us a daily cleansing from sin and, by incorporating us into Himself, imbued us with His own gentleness.

Sermon outline. Introduction: Discuss general theme for these Lenten sermons, "The Fruit of the Spirit," and its relation to Christ.

THE FRUIT OF THE SPIRIT IS GENTLENESS

I. Many people do not value gentleness highly.
   A. A gentle person may be regarded as weak, spineless, timid, or cowardly.
   B. Instead, a person ought to be aggressive, assert himself, stand up for his rights, take care of himself because nobody else will.
   C. Gentleness can look like a cop-out. A person can be too self-abasing. But that is not gentleness.
II. Jesus, the most beautiful person who ever lived, was gentle.
   A. He was gentle with people who deserved worse treatment.
   B. He was gentle even though He had all power and glory.
   C. Jesus served with gentleness to purify us from our sinful assertiveness.
III. We can be gentle.
   A. We show gentleness when we recognize and appreciate others.
   B. We show gentleness when we speak the truth out of loving concern for the person.
Conclusion: Left to ourselves, we'll always be harsh and hard. But we don't have to remain captives of our evil nature and of the behavior of the world around

us. We are not left to ourselves. The Holy Spirit is at work inside us to do what we can never do on our own. The fruit of the Spirit is gentleness.

Thematic approach. A theme derived from the text is developed in a coherent, unified, but also text-oriented way.

Sermon outline. Introduction: The world says: "Blessed are the aggressive." When Christ declares (v. 17), "Blessed are you if you do them," *them* refers to what has preceded, namely Christ's demonstration of gentleness toward His disciples. So Christ is saying

BLESSED ARE THE GENTLE

I. Our gentleness is evidence of our cleansing by Christ.
  A. Christ loved us so much He died for us to cleanse us from our sin.
  B. Because in Christ we are "clean all over," we are able to show others the gentleness Christ showed us.
II. Our gentleness is evidence of our imitation of Christ.
  A. The Christ who displayed no greedy ambition, no desire for reward, no spirit of vengeance
  B. The Christ who always respected the dignity of each person
Conclusion: Blessed be the Lord Christ, who served us all the way to a cross. Blessed are we who through Him produce the fruit of gentleness!

Metaphorical approach. The primary action in the text is utilized to shape the sermon into a metaphor that points to Christ's service culminating on the cross and to our service in response to Christ.

Sermon outline. Introduction: "Jesus knew that His hour had come to depart out of this world." Seemingly an inopportune time for foot washing. Didn't this crisis call for something more in tune with the disciples' foreboding, for action more in accord with Christ's position as Lord? Yet Jesus, just hours before His death, performed the task of a lowly slave. He didn't ask

ME? A FOOT WASHER?

I. Jesus did not come to be served but to serve.
  A. His service flowed from love which extended even to a Judas.
  B. His service manifested itself in His self-sacrifice on the cross.
II. The foot washing pointed to the supreme service of cleansing wrought on Calvary's cross.
  A. Through Christ's death we are cleansed from sin.
  B. Incorporated into Christ's death by Baptism, we have become foot washers.
III. What a privilege to be a foot washer!
  A. To reach out to others in love and concern
  B. To show others the gentleness Christ has shown us
Conclusion: Me? A foot washer? Such we have become in Christ. By His Spirit Christ helps us to be what we are, gentle servants—foot washers.

Sermon Illustrations

Greece said, "Be moderate; know thyself." Rome said, "Be strong; order thyself." Confucianism says, "Be superior; correct thyself." Buddhism says, "Be disillusioned; annihilate thyself." Mohammedanism says, "Be submissive; bend thyself." Modern materialism says, "Be industrious; enjoy thyself." Modern dilettantism says, "Be broad; cultivate thyself." Christianity says, "Be Christlike; give thyself." (From *Windows, Ladders and Bridges* by A. Dudley Dennison Jr., M.D. Copyright © 1976 by the Zondervan Corporation. Used by permission)

A pressure cooker keeps building up steam until finally something must give way. An open pot gets just as much heat, yet the steam escapes as quickly as it is generated. Meekness is like the open pot. It harbors no explosive temper, no anger, no grudges, no resentments, no wounded feelings, no frustrations. (Paul G. Bretscher, "The Fruit of the Spirit Is Meekness," *The Lutheran Witness,* October 28, 1952, p. 3)

A pin prick can explode a balloon only when it is inflated .... Meekness is a perfect safety valve against emotional strain and tension. (Bretscher, "Meekness," p. 3)

"Blessed are the meek," says Jesus, "for they shall inherit the earth."...

To the world....no statement of the Lord is more patently ridiculous than this one....Any Christian who takes this call to meekness too literally will be left far behind in the dust....No man concerned with ordinary bread-and-butter security can operate on such a principle. "Blessed are the aggressive!" That's the way life is, and that's how it must be lived...."Don't be such a milktoast," the aggressive wife prods her reluctant husband. "Don't be such a spineless weakling! For once in your life stand up for your rights. Tell him where to head in. If you are so chickenhearted, people will continue to walk all over you."

"Blessed is the man who knows what he wants and sets out to get it, who has the courage to assert himself, to defend his rights, press his claims, demand his due"....

....God needs a people in this perverted world who will be meek. Such people will so trust Him that they on the one hand will want to serve their neighbor rather than dominate him. On the other hand such people will have the courage to absorb the shocks of those who seek security and life by dominating others, and who thereby perpetuate every kind of sin and injustice. (Paul G. Bretscher, *The World Upside Down or Right Side Up* [St. Louis: CPH, 1964], pp. 36-44)

Meekness is real strength — Moses, Abraham, Paul.

Lent 2

Patience in Light of Matt. 26:36-46

Word Study of Patience

Usage in secular Greek. The word *makrothumia* in some contexts contains a certain element of resignation. In other contexts it suggests delay or procrastination, the putting off of an action. It is used also in a good sense, however, for the patience of a physician in treating severe illnesses with only small hope of a cure, for the steadfastness of the soldier who puts up with hardships, and for perseverance in one's work or in the battle of life.

Old Testament usage. The word takes on a distinctive depth in Biblical usage. The divine attitude has become indissolubly linked with *makrothumia* so that the human attitude is set in a new light. The formula of Ex. 34:6 echoes again and again through the Old Testament.

The patience of God is displayed in His forgiveness. This is the bridge that leads to the requirement of patience from man. Man should not allow his anger to break forth, but he should restrain it, considering the work of God.

The new attitude to which man is brought by the patience of God will show itself on the one hand in his exercising patience towards his neighbor and on the other hand in his learning to understand the affliction he experiences as a test that teaches him patience and directs him to God. Thus patience is a gift of God, not an arbitrary cultivation of the virtue by man.

New Testament usage. In the parable of the wicked servant in Matt. 18:23-35, the *makrothumia* of God consists essentially in the full readiness of forgiving grace. Now it is expected that the man who has really taken it seriously will be altered in his own attitude to his fellows. Patience toward men springs from a new relationship to God in which the believer has understood the *makrothumia* of God.

Another feature of the *makrothumia* of God in the New Testament is its decidedly eschatological reference. In the parable of the importunate widow (Luke 18:1-8a), the tension in which believers stand between the promise of a speedy vindication and the need to pray for the coming of God's kingdom finds its solution in the saying *kai makrothumei ep autois* (and be patient over them). God's patience is for the harassed elect a necessary interval of grace which should kindle their faith and prayer.

In 1 Thess. 5:14 Paul echoes the Synoptists when he points out that God's patient dealings with Christians must find expression in their mutual correction of each other in patience. This patience is not merely a virtue among other virtues but a fruit of the Spirit (Gal. 5:22) and is controlled by love. In Col. 1:11 patience is a necessary part of the Christian walk, no mere endurance, but a specifically spiritual force.

In James 5:7-11 patience is orientated to expectation of the Parousia. Christ's nearness quenches angry feelings against opponents and all hasty murmurings against brothers since both parties will stand against this Judge.

Text Study of Matt. 26:36-46

General setting of text. The many Jewish terms and references to Jewish matters in Matthew's gospel indicate that Matthew was concerned especially about connecting the New Testament with the Old. His theme seems to be that Jesus, the Messiah and Savior of the world, is the Christ promised to David and to Abraham before him. The great number of Old Testament quotations is in line with this general theme. The greater part of the gospel consists of discourses, and there is a mass of detail. While Matthew follows the general chronological order, he groups some details according to their character and significance.

Immediate context. The preceding verses (vv. 20-30) contain Matthew's account of the Last Supper with Jesus' reference to Judas the betrayer. In verse 30 we are told that they left the Upper Room and went to the Mount of Olives, where Jesus says to the disciples that they will all fall away and forsake Him that night. Peter then counters that though all others will or might forsake Him, he will not, that even if he has to die with Him, he will not deny Him. The other disciples join in saying the same thing (v. 35). In the verses immediately following the text (47-50), Judas enters the garden, leading the mob, and betrays Jesus with a kiss. The same incidents precede and follow in the parallel account in Mark 14:32-42 and in Luke 22:40-46, except that between Peter's avowal and the entrance to Gethsemane Luke inserts Jesus' discussion of the need to now take along not only a purse but a bag as well as a sword (vv. 35-38).

Text in vernacular. Vv. 37-38 "My soul is exceeding sorrowful, even unto death" (KJV) "...began to be in terrible pain and agony of mind. 'My heart is breaking with a death-like grief' " (Phillips). "Anguish and dismay came over Him, and He said to them, 'My heart is ready to break with grief,' " (NEB). "...began to be grieved and distressed. Then He said to them, 'My soul is deeply grieved to the point of death,' " (NAS). "Grief and anguish came over Him, and He said to them, 'The sorrow in My heart is so great that it almost crushes Me'" (TEV). "He started to feel sad and troubled. Then He said to them, 'My soul is so full of sorrow I am almost dying'" (Beck).

V. 41 "Your spirit is willing, but human nature is weak" (Phillips). All the other translations have, "but the flesh is weak."

V. 45 "Are you still sleeping and taking your ease?" (Phillips). "Still sleeping? Still taking your ease? The hour has come!" (NEB). "Are you still sleeping and taking your rest?" (NAS). "Are you going to sleep on now and rest?" (Beck). "Are you still sleeping and resting?" (TEV).

Text in original. V. 36. Gethsemane means oil press in the Hebrew, or olive vat. Jesus entered Gethsemane with 11 disciples and then took 3 of the disciples with Him deeper into the orchard. He went for a short distance even from Peter, James, and John to pray.

V. 37. The Greek word *ademonein* at the end of the verse means, literally, sorely troubled or dismayed. The word seems to be used of the dismay that comes with an unexpected calamity. Mark says that Christ was sore amazed (*ekthambeisthai*) or greatly amazed (14:33). It is as though the prospect of what was coming suddenly opened up to Him and overwhelmed Him. All that He would have to undergo now presented itself to His human consciousness, and the burden was crushing.

V. 38. Christ speaks in strong language of sorrow unto death, words that ought to have alarmed the disciples. Here Jesus alludes to a mental agony. He was not thinking only of the bodily pain He faced but of all that had led to His passion, that would accompany it, and that would succeed it. He was beginning to submit Himself to the punishment of sin, tasting death for every man, bearing in His own person the iniquity that the Lord had laid upon Him, becoming sin on our behalf (2 Cor. 5:21). As a man He yearned for the comfort of other men. Even though Peter, James, and John would not witness the extremity of His agony, yet their proximity and sympathy and prayers would be a support. It did not seem too much to ask.

V. 39. What transpires now is explained in Heb. 5:7-8.

V. 40. There is a tone of sad disappointment at the discovery that they were asleep after the earnest plea that they keep awake (v. 38). Luke says that the disciples were "sleeping for sorrow." Poignant distress often produces bodily stupor and sleep. Yet this was not a valid excuse for such insensibility in this terrible crisis. But Christ's reproach is tender.

V. 41. Watch and pray. Jesus repeats the command of verse 38 with the addition of prayer and with the warning against the peril of temptation. He Himself was feeling the worst of all temptations of His life just then. The disciples' weakness was due to weakness of the flesh. Here note the contrast between the spirit and the body. The disciples had shown a certain readiness of spirit when they offered to die for Christ (v. 35), but the flesh, the lower nature, represses the higher impulse, checks the will, and prevents it from carrying out what it would like to do.

V. 42. Christ accepts the cup; His human will coincides with the divine will. He knew that the cup could not pass.

V. 43. He was still yearning for sympathy and desirous of their safety under temptation. But they were weighed down with drowsiness. He aroused them partially, but they were too overcome with sleep to enter fully into the situation.

V. 44. His prayer was the same now a third time, whereby He obtained strength to submit, endure, and conquer.

V. 45. Jesus has won the victory without their aid. His time of weakness is past, and He is prepared to face the worst. Now He allows His fatigued followers to sleep on till the last moment.

Doctrinal study. The divine-human nature of Christ. His humiliation. Law: cup of suffering on account of sin; flesh weak; temptations come; watch. Gospel: readiness to drink the cup; tender patience with disciples; facing the ordeal of the cross.

Parallel passages. Ps. 42:5; John 6:38; 2 Cor. 1:3-5; 4:8-10.

Central thought. Jesus shows patience when He submits to suffering and also when he reproves the sleeping disciples.

Homiletical Treatment

Goal-malady-means approach. The goal is that the hearers will learn from and find in Jesus patience for their trying situations. The malady is that we feel obstacles must be eliminated right now. The means to achieve the goal is Jesus' patient endurance of suffering which enables us to wait on God's timetable.

Sermon outline.

THE FRUIT OF THE SPIRIT IS PATIENCE

I. Impatience is a problem for us all.
  A. We become angry, sarcastic, or harsh toward another person because the person offended us or failed to do what we wanted him or her to do.
  B. We become bitter and rebellious in our sufferings.
  C. We become tense and anxious because other people and our sufferings prevent us from getting done what we would like to do.
II. The Spirit helps us to be patient.
  A. The Spirit reminds us that God has been and still is patient with us.
  B. The Spirit reminds us that suffering is never meaningless.
  C. The Spirit reminds us that we have all eternity to get our work done.
Conclusion: Impatience is built into us as human beings. But we don't have to be discouraged. We can grow in patience because patience is the fruit of the Spirit.

Thematic approach. The sermon is shaped by the interplay of the text with the hymn, "Go to Dark Gethsemane."

Sermon outline. Introduction: In Gethsemane Jesus drank a cup of agony in which He saw humanity in all its alienation from God. That alienation Jesus felt in His own soul. He endured an inner cross that anticipated the cross on Golgatha. What Jesus experienced in Gethsemane He experienced for us. That is why we do well to

GO TO DARK GETHSEMANE

I. Your Redeemer's conflict see.
  A. A conflict brought on by our sin
  B. A conflict which alone could redeem us from sin
II. Watch with Him one bitter hour.
  A. Learn from Him to submit to God's will
  B. Find in Him the patience you need
Conclusion: Gethsemane tells of redemptive conflict and patient watchfulness,

of forgiveness for past failures, and of power to stay awake. Christ's patience with us enables us to be patient with God, with others, and with ourselves.

Narrative approach. The story of the text is told in such a way as to focus on the Gospel story and to incorporate the hearers' stories.

Sermon outline. Introduction: We've all known people who were not alert to the dangers threatening their faith life and who eventually lost their Christian faith.

ARE WE WATCHING?

I. Jesus' request that we watch is not unreasonable.
   A. In His terrible anguish He craved the support of His friends.
   B. He does not ask us to do what He hasn't already done—to watch that our will conforms to God's will.
II. Yet we have difficulty watching.
   A. Temptations to sin are strong.
   B. Our sinful flesh is weak, and thus we lapse into indifference, cockiness, and spiritual sleep.
III. Christ's patience encourages us to watch.
   A. There was no putdown or bawling out of the disciples.
   B. Christ patiently suffered for them and for us in Gethsemane and on the cross, atoning for all our failures to watch.
   C. Christ patiently supports us so that we can remain spiritually alert.
Conclusion: It requires patience to keep watching against dangers that threaten our faith life. Patience is possible in Christ.

Sermon Illustrations

A woman, a former surgeon on the staff of the hospital where she now lay as a patient, told me, "This may sound strange to you, Pastor, but I thank God for giving me tuberculosis these last thirty months. In the last ten years, although I was brought up in the church, I had totally forgotten about God in my daily life. Lying on my back these many months has given me plenty of opportunity to re-examine my faith and to get my feet planted again, with God's help, on the road back to God."

Thank God for tuberculosis? It sounds strange, but perhaps the secret is locked up in the rest of the passage..., "We glory in tribulations also, knowing that tribulation worketh patience; and patience, experience; and experience, hope; and hope maketh not ashamed because the love of God is shed abroad in our hearts by the Holy Ghost, which is given unto us" (Rom. 5:3-5 KJV).

Ah, there is the key! The love of God will give us the patience. God knows what He is doing, even though we cannot understand it now. (Donald L. Deffner, *Bold Ones on Campus* [St. Louis: CPH, 1973], pp. 106-7)

Imagine a father who has just returned home from another business trip. He is impatient to share the details of his trip with his wife. His smallest child is hanging on his left trouser leg. His son is pounding on the piano. The radio and the TV are both on. The wife is hectically preparing dinner. An older daughter can't stop talking to her mother about the new clothes she's making.

Patience, Father! Remember your calling as a father and source of strength for your family involves not just getting your own needs and ego trips satisfied!

Count your blessings! (From *The Best of Your Life Is the Rest of Your Life* by Donald L. Deffner, p. 44. Copyright© 1977 by Abingdon; used by permission)

In his book *Creative Brooding* Robert Raines relates the story of a boy who left home because he had always gotten material things from his parents. What he really wanted was for them to just listen to him as somebody who felt things too....

Who is there in my life today who needs the patience, the time, and the love that I can give them? (Deffner, *Best of Your Life,* pp. 45-46)

Fabre, the greatest naturalist who ever lived, began the main part of his work at 60; he was able to give all his time to it when he was 70; and he was discovered by fame at the age of 90. He had done all of his work without a laboratory; all of his insects had been raised in old flowerpots and sardine cans. He always referred to his two best instruments as time and patience.

God tells us that He uses these two things in developing our spiritual lives. How many times we are told to wait upon the Lord! The flesh does not want to take time, but God does because He is dealing with eternity.

Faithfulness in Light of Matt. 26:47-56

Word Study of Faithfulness

Usage in secular Greek. Pistis means confidence or trust in relation to persons and things. It can denote not only the confidence one has but the confidence one enjoys, that is, trustworthiness. The fact is often stressed that *pistis* is a higher endowment than wealth.

Pistis did not become a specifically religious term in classical Greek. It can, however, refer to reliance on a god. The word *pisteuein* can mean "to put faith" in not only human words but also divine sayings and even deity itself. The use of *pistis* as a religious term was promoted by the fact that it became a catchword not only in Christianity but in all religions that proclaimed their message to gain adherents.

Old Testament usage. In the Old Testament, for the most part, anthropological interest is secondary to a theocentric view. As the Old Testament understands it, faith is always man's reaction to God's primary action. Man's reaction manifests itself specifically as reliance on God's promises and praise to God for His mighty deeds.

When the reference of the Old Testament word for faith is to God, it comprises many different aspects: His might, His miraculous power, His electing will, His love, the steadfastness and faithfulness of His conduct, the actualizing of His Word and plan, His demand, His righteousness. The stress is on taking God as God with unremitting seriousness.

At the same time, faith in the Old Testament denotes a relation to God that embraces the whole man in the totality of his external conduct and inner life. This relation to God excludes any autonomy on man's part or any commitment to other gods. God initiated a covenant with Israel in which He bestowed on Israel His forgiving grace. Every person in Israel was expected to demonstrate his faith in God's covenant by ordering his entire life daily according to God's commands.

This Old Testament understanding of faith is clearly seen in Isaiah. He differentiates faith from political considerations (7:1f.) and from trust in human might (30:15f.). Faith for Isaiah is a particular form of existence of those who are bound to God. The man of faith puts his confidence in God's mercy, commits his life into God's keeping, and humbly serves God as his Redeemer and Lord.

These actions on man's part exhibit man's faithfulness. The Hebrew term for faithfulness is *'āman.* In Num. 12:7 it refers to the faithfulness of Moses; in Deut. 7:9, to the faithfulness of God.

New Testament usage. Pistis can mean both "faithfulness" and "trust," though it is seldom used in the sense of faithfulness. In Rom. 3:3 it is used of the faithfulness of God. Faithfulness in human dealings is referred to in Matt. 23:23, in Titus 2:10, and, of course, in Gal. 5:22. In 1 Tim. 5:12 the Greek term is translated "pledge" in the RSV and almost means oath. In Acts 17:31 *pistin* means "to give a pledge," "to offer proof."

In *pistis* as faithfulness there is an echo of the Old Testament sense of faithfulness. In Rev. 2:13 where the church at Pergamum is praised for not denying "my faith," faithfulness is implied. Heb. 11:17 tells us that faith proves itself as faithfulness in temptation. In 1 Peter *pistis* is seen to be the faithfulness that must be demonstrated when tested.

To be distinguished from all other senses of *pistis* is the specifically Christian use of the term seen most clearly in the formula *pistis eis,* which is to be understood as acceptance of the Christian kerygma. It is thus the saving faith which recognizes and appropriates God's saving work in Christ. Trust, hope, and faithfulness are also implied. In the specifically Christian concept of *pistis,* faith looks primarily to what God has done in Christ, not to what He will do.

Insofar as faith itself is faithfulness, it is faithfulness to the saving act in Christ, to the one name in which is salvation (Acts 4:12). Faithfulness, steadfastness in faith, must be displayed in all temptations, and especially in persecution.

Text Study of Matt. 26:47-56

General setting of text. See preceding text study.

Immediate context. The text of the preceding sermon immediately precedes this text, while the following verses (57f.) relate what happened when Jesus was brought before Caiaphas.

Text in vernacular. Vv. 49-50. "Without any hesitation he walked up to Jesus. 'Greetings, Master!' he cried, and kissed Him affectionately" (Phillips). "And stepping forward at once, he said, 'Hail, Rabbi!', and kissed Him. Jesus replied, 'Friend, do what you are here to do'" (NEB). "And immediately he came to Jesus and said, 'Hail, Rabbi!' and kissed Him. And Jesus said to him, 'Friend, do what you have come for'" (NAS). "Judas went straight to Jesus and said, 'Peace be with You, Teacher,' and kissed Him. Jesus answered, 'Be quick about it, friend!'" (TEV).

V. 53. "...12 armies of angels" (TEV). "...70,000 angels to help Me" (Beck). All the rest have "12 legions of angels."

V. 54. "How, then, could the Bible be true when it says this must happen?" (Beck). "But in that case, how could the Scriptures come true which say that this is what must happen?" (TEV). "But then, how would the Scriptures be fulfilled which say that all this must take place?" (Phillips).

Text in original. V. 47. Judas is described as "one of the Twelve" here and in all three synoptic gospels (Mark 14:43; Matt. 26:47; Luke 22:47). The horror of the thing is thus emphasized, that one of the chosen twelve should betray Him. He was accompanied by a "great multitude" *(ochlos polus)*. Judas was taking no chances, for he knew the strange power of Jesus.

V. 48. In the East the kiss was a common salutation among friends, master, and pupils. What audacity and obduracy to employ this mark of affection and respect to signal an act of treachery!

V. 50. Christ endeavors by kindness and love to win Judas over still. There is uncertainty in this verse as to whether Christ is asking a question or uttering an exclamation. It can be seen as both a question and an exclamation. "Why are you here?" can be taken as a last remonstrance and appeal to Judas's conscience. It could also be taken as an imperative, as in the NAS: "Friend, *do* what you have come for." At any rate, Jesus exposes the pretense of Judas.

V. 51. Like the other Synoptists, Matthew conceals the name of Peter, while John reveals it (John 18:10). The servant's name, Malchus, is given by John (18:10). The disciples had misunderstood the Lord's words uttered a little while before about him who has no sword selling his cloak and buying one (Luke 22:36-38). Physical courage Peter had, but moral courage he and the other disciples lacked when they all forsook Him and fled (v. 56). Evidently Peter intended to cut off the man's head, but the blow fell short. How the wound was healed is related only by Luke.

V. 52. Jesus sternly rebukes Peter. Those who arbitrarily resort to violence will themselves feel violence.

V. 53. The verb translated with give is a military term meaning "to place by the side," "to post on one's flank." So the Lord implies that at a word the ranks of angels would range themselves at His side to defend and support Him. He employs the Roman term *legion*. He has been arrested by a cohort, the 10th part of a legion which numbered 6,000 men (John 18:3, 12). He could, if He chose, call to His aid 12 times 6,000 angels who would deliver Him from His enemies. And who could withstand those heavenly hosts?

V. 55. All the past week Christ had taught quietly and openly in the temple. He had not acted the way a robber acts. He had not done things in secret. Why should a company of armed men now come to arrest Him?

V. 56. But all this was done that the Scriptures might be fulfilled. He remained faithful to his Father and to the Father's Word.

Doctrinal study. Law: Believers can be faithless (v. 56b). Gospel: Jesus to the end seeks to call back the sinner (v. 50); He will not use His almighty power, for He wishes to redeem men in accordance with the Scriptures (vv. 53-54). He is faithful to His Father and to the Scriptures despite the faithlessness of His own (v. 56).

Parallel passages. The Gospel parallels are Mark 14:43-50; Luke 22:47-53; and John 18:2-11. Other parallel passages are Ps. 119:50; Prov. 27:6; Hos. 2:20; Matt. 4:11; 23:27; 25:21; John 1:9; 19:26-27; Acts 11:23; Rom. 3:3; 1 Cor. 1:9, 10:13; and Heb. 3:6.

Central thought. Despite the faithlessness of Judas, Jesus remains faithful to His Father and to His own.

Homiletical Treatment

Goal-malady-means approach. The goal is that the hearers will have a sense of responsibility to God and to people. The malady is that we fail to use our abilities and talents conscientiously. The means to the goal is the faithfulness of Christ, which makes up for our faithlessness and promises us the gift of faithfulness.

Sermon outline. Introduction: We sometimes say about an air conditioner, power mower, or car that it performs faithfully. We mean that it has given us years of trouble-free service. When we say of another person that he or she is faithful, we mean that that person has conscientiously carried out his or her responsibilities. We all have responsibilities as husbands or wives, parents or children, employers or employees, and as members of a church and citizens of a country. The gift of the Spirit that enables us to carry out our responsibilities resolutely and conscientiously is faithfulness.

THE FRUIT OF THE SPIRIT IS FAITHFULNESS

I. Sometimes faithlessness is more evident than faithfulness.
   A. Judas became faithless in his responsibilities as treasurer.
   B. The disciples were faithless in not giving Christ the support He needed in His suffering.
   C. Fidelity is synonymous with faithfulness and is used in Gal. 5:22 by Phillips and by the NEB. It's a sad commentary on present-day thinking that the word *fidelity* is used almost entirely in speaking of technical equipment, such as amplifiers and speakers for stereophonic sound. We hardly ever see it or hear it used of people.
II. Jesus was completely faithful.
   A. He was faithful to His disciples.
   B. He was faithful to His heavenly Father.
   C. His faithfulness makes up for our faithlessness; it covers it, atones for it.
III. Now we can show faithfulness.
   A. We show faithfulness by keeping our commitment to Christ.
   B. We show faithfulness by living with a sense of responsibility to others (the "do your own thing" philosophy knows nothing of commitment to others.)

Conclusion: We are not in ourselves faithful by nature. But we do not live the Christian life by ourselves but by the power of the Holy Spirit. The fruit of the Spirit is faithfulness.

Thematic Approach. Important incidents and ideas in the text are employed to develop a general theme deduced from the text.

Sermon outline. Introduction: It's surprising that Jesus had enemies. He was pure and holy. No one had even been able to accuse Him of sin. Yet there were people who hated Him and wanted nothing to do with Him. Our text describes Jesus' encounter with His enemies. What stands out in this encounter is

THE FAITHFULNESS OF JESUS

I. Jesus was faithful toward His disciples.
   A. It's incredible that He still called Judas "friend."
   B. Although our faithlessness, like that of the disciples (v. 56), is not in the same category as Judas's betrayal, it is still sinful behavior.
   C. Jesus nevertheless regards us as His friends (John 15:5).

II. Jesus was faithful toward His heavenly Father.
   A. He refused to meet violence with violence (v. 52).
   B. He resisted the temptation to call for a spectacular deliverance (v. 53).
   C. His concern was to fulfil the Scriptures (vv. 54, 56), which foretold His betrayal and His deliverance into evil hands, all for the purpose of securing the world's redemption.

Conclusion: How reassuring to know that our faithlessness does not nullify His faithfulness!

Monologue approach. A dramatic monologue by Judas urges faithfulness by pointing to Judas's own sad experience and to Christ's utter faithfulness.

Sermon outline. Introduction: You despise a person who becomes a traitor to his country. You cringe at the word *betrayer.* Although I am known as the most despicable betrayer of all, let me have a few moments of your time.

I AM JUDAS

I. Once I was a disciple of Jesus.
   A. I responded with joy to Christ's call to follow Him.
   B. There were high hopes for me, as there were for you at your baptism and your confirmation.

II. But I became a betrayer of Jesus.
   A. I gave in to covetousness. Despite warnings from Jesus, that sin gained control of me.
   B. You have the right to condemn me. But also ask yourself whether you are betraying Jesus by failing to confess Him, by failing to do what He has called you to do, to carry out your responsibilities as a church member, a parent, a spouse, or a child.

III. I ended up as a child of perdition.
   A. Christ's last desperate appeal to me did not get through. I had set my plan. Later, when I was sorry for what I did, I could not bring myself to believe that Christ could forgive me.
   B. You may think you have been sadly unfaithful to Christ, that you have betrayed Him shamefully. Don't do as I did. Don't be afraid to turn to Jesus. With Him there is plenteous forgiveness. Jesus promises: "Him who comes to Me, I will not cast out" (John 6:37). "I forgive you all your sins."

Sermon Illustrations

George D. Marler maintains that Old Faithful, that marvelous Yellowstone National Park geyser, has never missed an eruption.

The reason is simple: Unlike an airline or railroad timetable, geysers depart only when they're ready, not when someone has calculated they should be. The time between eruptions varies; it depends on a number of factors, including the duration of the previous eruption. But you can count on Old Faithful to erupt sometime between 38 and 90 minutes from the last eruption.

God's love is even more faithful than that. It never ceases to shower the penitent with forgiveness and peace—and it never depends on how much He gave the last time. (Donald L. Deffner and Richard Andersen, *For Example* [St. Louis: CPH, 1977], p. 93)

If your car starts one out of three times, do you consider it faithful?

If the paper boy skips the Monday and Thursday editions, are they missed?

If you fail to come to work two or three times a month, does your boss call you faithful? If your refrigerator quits for a day now and then, do you excuse it and say, "Oh well, it works most of the time?"

If your water heater greets you with cold water once in a while, do you call it faithful?

If you miss a couple of mortgage payments a year, does the loan company say, "Oh well, 10 out of 12 isn't bad?" If you fail to worship God in church one or two Sundays a month, are you faithful?

God gave us not only the living water—He gives us a *jug* of living water. The Spirit gave us faith—and as a special fruit of the faith He gives faithfulness, a life of faith....

Faithfulness is the jug that allows us to carry our faith with us in all we do. It is a jug that is never emptied, because the more we apply our faith to our daily living, the more powerful and more refreshing our faith becomes. (Eldon Weisheit, "The Fruit of the Spirit Is Faithfulness," *The Lutheran Witness*, April 7, 1974, p. 5)

I must use my gifts according to the will of God, in a way that will help to carry out His good and gracious purpose through me. That is stewardship in the widest sense of the term. Paul writes: "It is required in stewards that a man be found faithful." (1 Cor. 4:2 KJV)

Where husband and wife live together in love and companionship, sharing their joys and sorrows; where children love, honor, and respect their parents; where parents regard children as a gift of God entrusted to their care; where relatives, friends, acquaintances, meet one another with trust and good will; where [people] do the work of their job or profession not merely to make a living but for the greater welfare of many; where money and goods are looked upon not as personal possessions but as a trust to be administered for the greater good it may do; where members of a community, a state, a nation, strive for justice...[and] good will; where church members realize the dignity of their calling—there [we see] faithfulness to God and [to people]. (E. W. Luecke, "Fruit of the Spirit—Faithfulness," *The Lutheran Witness*, October 14, 1952, p. 3)

Goodness in Light of Matt. 26:57-68

Word Study of Goodness

Usage in secular Greek. As an adjective *agathos* means excellent, fine, good. Applied to persons, it signifies the excellence of the person in his existing position. Applied to things, it signifies the good quality of the thing referred to. Substantively, it denotes the good or goods, that is, the things that relate to man's well-being.

Old Testament usage. In the Old Testament the idea of the good in the Greek and the Hellenistic sense is not present. The term *good* is applied to God as a perfectly good being (1 Chron. 16:34), but it is a personal God to whom goodness is attributed. In His goodness God established a covenant with Israel "for their own good and the good of their children after them" (Jer. 32:39), and in the eschatological future God will "bring upon them all the good" that He promised them (Jer. 32:42). Between the establishment of the covenant and its fulfilment in Messianic salvation, God requires of man what is good, namely, to do justly, to love mercy, and to walk humbly before the Lord (Micah 6:8).

New Testament usage. Jesus in Matt. 19:17 ("One there is who is good") reiterates the Old Testament declaration about God. Here the term *good* expresses the essential goodness of God.

From this God there comes the salvation which is the central idea in the New Testament. It is in this sense of salvation that the term is used in Heb. 9:11.

The natural existence of man is excluded from the good and cannot attain to it in spite of every longing. According to Paul, in the Law a good is certainly given to man (Rom. 7:12f.). But the sin that possesses and controls man, which is the reality of his existence, works death for him through the Law. So the New Testament view of life sees man hopelessly delivered up to death and sin to a sphere in which there is no possibility of goodness or salvation.

With the revelation of salvation in Christ a radically new possibility of life is introduced (Rom. 12:2). It may be said of Christians that "we are His workmanship, created in Christ Jesus for good works, which God prepared beforehand, that we should walk in them" (Eph. 2:10), and that we are "to lead a life worthy of the Lord, fully pleasing to Him, bearing fruit in every good work" (Col. 1:10a). According to 1 Thess. 5:15 the good is achieved in concrete person-to-person and person-to-God relationships. This new possibility of existence is the meaning of the life of a Christian.

A Christian who grasps this new possibility has the good conscience of which Paul speaks in Acts 23:1 and in 1 Tim. 1:5 and 19. At the same time the Christian has the certainty that salvation is the goal of his life (Rom. 8:28). Paul's statement in Phil. 1:6 comprehends the whole Christian understanding of life.

The word *agathōsunē* as found in Gal. 5:22 has come down from the LXX into the New Testament and the Greek of the church. It indicates the quality a man has who is *agathos*—moral excellence as well as goodness. Its posession constitutes the content of the life of the Christian (Rom. 15:14; 2 Thess. 1:11).

Text Study of Matt. 26:57-68

General setting of text. This has been commented on sufficiently in preceding studies.

Immediate context. The preceding verses have already been commented on in the text study of faithfulness. The following verses (69f., Peter's denial) constitute the text for the next sermon dealing with self-control.

Text in vernacular. V. 64. "Thou hast said" (KJV). "You have said so" (RSV). "You have said so" (Phillips). "The words are yours" (NEB). "You have said it yourself" (NAS). "I am" (Beck). "Yes, it is as you say," Jesus replied. "But I say to all of you: In the future..." (NIV). "So you say" (TEV).

TEV continues: "But I tell all of you: from this time on you will see...." Beck: "But I tell you, from now on you will all see...." NAS has: "nevertheless I tell you, hereafter you shall see...." Phillips: "Yes, and I tell you that in the future you will see...." NEB: "But I tell you this: from now on, you will see the Son of Man...." RSV and KJV: "hereafter you will see...."

In the rest of the verses there is no significant variation in the English translations.

Text in original. V. 57. Led Him to Caiaphas the high priest. The Synoptists omit all mention of the preliminary inquiry before Annas (John 18:13; 19:24). Members of the Sanhedrin had been hastily convened for an informal meeting in a chamber of Caiaphas's palace.

V. 59. Sought false testimony against Jesus. *Ezētoun* is the imperfect, "kept on seeking." Judges have no right to be prosecutors, least of all to seek after false witnesses and even to offer bribes to those witnesses. But they had already made up their minds that Christ should be killed. Now they just had to find a charge against Him that would compel the Roman authorities to deal with Him. The truth of the accusation was immaterial so long as it was established according to law by two or three witnesses examined apart.

V. 60. They found false witnesses but none that would stand the test.

V. 61. Finally, when the case seemed hopeless, they found two who distorted Christ's words about the temple of His body (John 2:19), and even those two didn't quite agree (Mark 14:59).

V. 63. Jesus held His peace. He was keeping silent (imperfect tense); He refused to answer the bluster of Caiaphas. He knew it was no use at this moment to explain the mystery of the words He had used relating to the temple. Puzzled and embarrassed by Christ's persistent silence, Caiaphas puts to Him a question that He has to answer. Putting Jesus on oath to make Him incriminate Himself was unlawful in Jewish law.

V. 64. The expression *su eipas* is an affirmative reply in the Greek. Mark 14:62 has it plainly, "I am," *Egō eimi*. But Jesus goes on to say that the day will come when He will be the Judge and Caiaphas the culprit. Jesus uses the prophetic language of Dan. 7:13 and Ps. 109:1.

Plēn is best translated "nevertheless" or "what is more." From this moment, beginning from now, from My suffering, My triumph and My reign are inaugurated. You, the representatives of Israel, will see the events about to take place that will prelude the coming of Messiah's kingdom. The reference to the right hand of power and to coming in the clouds of heaven asserts Christ's deity, and so He applied to Himself Ps. 110:1 and Dan. 7:13-14.

V. 65. Probably Caiaphas was relieved to find that the prisoner had saved him the trouble of seeking any more witnesses.

V. 66. Death was the penalty of blasphemy according to Lev. 24:15.

V. 67 and V. 68. Like hoodlums, these doctors of divinity insulted Jesus, spitting in His face, striking Him with their fists, and slapping Him with the palms of their hands. They gave vent to their spite and hatred of Him with incredible personal indignities.

Doctrinal study. Law: Evil men do not care what means they use to perpetrate their wickedness; they will resort to lies and bribery. They will disregard all the accepted rules of procedure. They lose all sense of human decency and act like savages. Jesus will one day be their Judge (v. 64). Gospel: Jesus suffers in silence for the sins of all people. His great goodness is for our benefit so that we are acceptable to Him when He comes to judge. Jesus is the almighty Son of God.

Parallel passages. Gospel parallels are Mark 14:53-72; Luke 22:54-71; John 18:12-27. Other parallel passages are Ps. 110:1; Dan. 7:13-14; Matt. 16:27.

Central thought. Even though Caiaphas resorted to evil, Jesus reveals divine goodness that accrues to our benefit.

Homiletical Treatment

Goal-malady-means approach. The goal is that the hearers will practice goodness the way God has been good to them. The malady is that our goodness is not always motivated by God's goodness. The means to the goal is that Christ who has made us good by His suffering and death empowers us by His Spirit to do good.

Sermon outline.

THE FRUIT OF THE SPIRIT IS GOODNESS

I. There doesn't seem to be much goodness in the world.
   A. Look at the evil perpetrated by Caiaphas and the Sanhedrin.
   B. Look at the evil in the world today.
II. Yet there is a kind of goodness in the world.
   A. This goodness is associated with outward deeds.

B. But the motivation of these deeds is not considered.
III. Real goodness is a fruit of the Spirit.
    A. There is no goodness apart from God and God's Spirit.
    B. The goodness that is a fruit of the Spirit is not merely a condition but a moving forth.

Conclusion: We are good people because we are God's people.

Thematic approach. The sharp contrast between good and evil in the text is utilized to develop a thematic outline which clearly sets forth the Law/Gospel dichotomy of the text.

Sermon outline. Introduction: We are faced with many questions. Both friends and enemies asked questions of Jesus and expected answers from Him. Caiaphas asked Jesus: "Have you no answer to make?" The text makes clear that

JESUS HAD AN ANSWER

  I. Jesus had an answer that condemned.
    A. Jesus by His silence condemned the travesty of justice that was being carried out.
    B. At times Jesus speaks no word of condemnation to us beyond what our conscience already tells us to be sin.
    C. The still small voice of our conscience is Christ's condemning answer to our self-seeking and superficial goodness.
  II. Jesus had an answer that saves.
    A. Jesus' answer pointed to Himself as the Christ who had come to remove our guilt and to secure goodness for us.
    B. Jesus' answer pointed to Himself as the One powerful enough to vanquish the forces of evil and to establish a kingdom of the good.
    C. Jesus' answer pointed to Himself as the One who would come at last to take all His believers into the heavenly kingdom of perfect goodness.

Conclusion. Life poses many questions we cannot answer. But when the chips are down, Christ's answer is all we need.

Textual-topical approach. A topic deduced from the text is developed independently of the text.

Sermon outline. Introduction: "Be good," we sometimes say to each other. We mean keep out of trouble, be reasonably honest, help someone out if you can. But is this being good?

WHAT MAKES US GOOD PEOPLE?

  I. We may think that a good cause makes us good regardless of the means we employ to further that cause. (The Jewish leaders thought their cause was good—better that Christ should die rather than that the whole nation should perish.)
    A. Have we sometimes resorted to lying and trumped up charges to further a cause we thought was right?
    B. Have we justified ridicule and mockery because the cause was good?

C. The end never justifies the means.
II. We may think that goodness consists of supporting good causes in ethical ways.
   A. No matter how ethical our actions, they still fall short of Christ's purity.
   B. The good we do, no matter how others praise it, still stands under Christ's judgment.
III. We are good only because of Christ's goodness imputed to us.
   A. This goodness alone is acceptable to God.
   B. The faith that receives Christ's goodness transforms us into good people who do deeds which, though imperfect, God accepts as good for Jesus' sake.
   C. When Christ comes on the last great day, we shall experience the eternal results of the goodness we have because Christ assumed our badness.

Sermon Illustrations

Goodness is a berry in the orchard of fruits of the Spirit....
Unfortunately, there is another berry called goodness in the lives of people.
...There is the goodness berry that grows on the bush of self-righteousness....
...Though the two berries may look alike at first glance, they grow on totally different bushes.
...All of us want to look good in the eyes of others. From childhood we are told, "Do good!" and "Be good!" We know that God has also told us to be good. This berry is a fruit of the law.
Could some of your "goodness" be fruits of the Law? Does your goodness condemn others? Is your goodness done to gain credit for yourself? Or to make up for some of the wrong you've done? (Eldon Weisheit, "The Fruit of the Spirit Is Goodness," *The Lutheran Witness,* March 7, 1974, p. 5)

There are three questions we ought to ask ourselves before we set out to be helpful to someone else: (1) Is what I am going to do in accordance with the Scriptures? (2) Does it avoid imposing my own will or interfering with the will of others? (3) Does it meet a genuine need, not only what I think is a need? (From *Learn to Live with Style* by Eileen Guder, p. 88. Copyright © 1978; used by permission of Word Books Publisher, Waco, Texas, 76796)

Many of Dixie's friends are elderly women. Dixie takes them shopping for groceries, out for Sunday drives, to doctor's appointments; she doesn't say much about what she's doing and I doubt if she thinks of it as "doing good." She is simply aware of the needs of these women most of us forget, and generous enough with her affection and her time to be a friend to them. (Guder, p. 76)

God's interest in making Christians is not aesthetic, but utilitarian. He has not fashioned us as spiritual objects of art. No, He has made us good *for* something. Our goodness is never an end in itself, but always a means for accomplishing God's purposes through our lives.... (Thomas Coates, "The Fruit of the Spirit Is Goodness," *The Lutheran Witness,* September 30, 1952, p. 3)

An old legend tells of Sir Launfal, the gallant knight who set out in quest of the Holy Grail, the chalice Christ used in celebrating the Last Supper. As the knight rode forth, he passed a leprous beggar by the wayside, who asked him for alms. Sir Launfal casually tossed him a gold coin and proceeded on his way. He was gone for years; he searched everywhere; but try as he would, he could not find the Holy Grail. Years later, haggard and dejected, he was returning home from the futile quest; and as he drew near the city, lo, the same beggar was still sitting by the wayside, still asking alms. But this time Sir Launfal stepped down from his horse, reached into his pouch, and drew out his last crust of bread to share with the beggar. Then, suddenly, miraculously, he beheld the Holy Grail. And from afar he heard the voice of Jesus: "Who gives himself with his gift feeds three: himself, his hungry neighbor, and me." (Coates, p. 3)

Self-control in Light of Matt. 26:69-75

Word Study of Self-control

Usage in secular Greek. The adjective *egkratēs* refers to one who has power over something and also one's self. *Egkrateia* then means the dominion that one has over one's self or something in the sense that one controls it. *Egkrateia* plays an important role in the philosophical ethics of classical Greece and Hellenism. It is reckoned a cardinal virtue by Socrates. For the Stoics it is associated with the free and independent man who is under no control but who freely controls all things and who in self-restraint maintains his freedom in the face of the forces that would deprive him of it.

For Philo *egkrateia* means a superiority expressed in restraint relating to food, sex, and the use of the tongue. It is linked with asceticism. Thus in Philo there is a shift of accent from the classical Greek view.

Old Testament usage. This term is not employed in the Old Testament. In the LXX it is most common in the Hellenistically influenced Wisdom literature.

New Testament usage. The word group is not found at all in the gospels. This is surprising when we remember that later schools have tried to see John the Baptist, for example, as an ascetic. On the other hand, Paul compares himself with the athlete who "exercises self-control in all things" (1 Cor. 9:25). Yet *egkrateia* here does not denote the asceticism of merit. It simply tells us that for the sake of the goal toward which he strives, the commission which he has been given, and the task which he must fulfil, he refrains from all the things that might offend or hamper. It is not for his own sake, or for the sake of any necessity to salvation, but for the sake of his brethren that he practices self-control. This is the fundamental difference from all the Greek and Hellenistic conceptions.

In 1 Cor. 7:9 the reference is to sexual restraint. Paul is concerned to protect the Christian from sexual defilement also in marriage. Yet that restraint in the ascetic sense is for him an alien concept.

It is striking how small a part this term plays in the Bible. The Biblical man saw the world with its gifts coming from the hand of the Creator. Also, the gift of salvation in Christ left no place for an asceticism that merits salvation.

Text Study of Matt. 26:69-75

General setting of text. Commented on sufficiently in preceding studies.

Immediate context. The immediately preceding verses describe the actions of Caiaphas and the Sandhedrin. Verse 58, however, really introduces the incident described in the text.

The verse immediately following (27:1) relates back to the conclusion of the council meeting in 26:66-68. Between the meeting at night when the Sanhedrin found Jesus guilty of blasphemy and the Good Friday morning meeting attended by probably a larger number of the Sanhedrin, Matthew has the episode of Peter's denial of Christ. Now, in the morning, the council was merely having to determine how they would formulate their charge against Jesus so that the Romans would be compelled to punish Him with death. Having decided the matter, they led Him away to Pilate. Then, verses 3-10 tell of Judas's remorse and his attempt to return the money. This transaction must have taken place either when Jesus was being conducted to the Praetorium or during the interview with Herod (Luke 22:7-11).

Text in vernacular. V. 74. "Then Peter said, 'I swear that I am telling the truth! May God punish me if I am not! I do not know that man!'" (TEV). "Then he began to call down curses on himself and he swore to them, 'I don't know the man!'" (NIV). "Then he began to invoke a curse on himself and to swear, 'I do not know the man'" (RSV).

All the other English versions have: "he began to curse and swear," or something very close to this. Otherwise there is no significant variation in the English versions.

Text in original. V. 69. Peter had gone within the palace but was sitting, outside the hall where the trial was going on, in the open central court with the servants or officers of the Sanhedrin. He could possibly see through the open door above what was going on inside. It is not plain at what stage of the trial the denials of Peter took place, nor the precise order in which the denials came, as the gospels give them variously. The maid who confronted Peter had probably noticed Peter come in with John. Or she may have seen him with Jesus on the streets of Jerusalem. Her word "also" was probably a reference to John, whom she let in first.

V. 71. Now Peter went into the porch, or the passage between the street and the court. Perhaps he wanted to escape further questioning. But here another maid (as well as a man, Luke 22:58) recognized him.

V. 72. This time Peter added an oath. He even referred to Jesus as "the man," an expression that could convey contempt, "the fellow."

V. 73. Apparently the talk about Peter continued. Luke 22:59 states that the little while was about an hour. The bystanders come up to Peter and bluntly assert that he of a truth is a follower of Jesus because his speech betrays him. The Greek has it simply, "makes you evident" (the Galileans had difficulty with the gutturals).

V. 74. Now he repeated his denial with the addition of profanity to prove that he was telling the truth instead of the lie they all knew. He called down imprecations in his desperate irritation and loss of self-control at his exposure.

V. 75. As the rooster crowed, Peter recalled the words of Jesus a few hours before to which he had uttered his proud boast (Matt. 26:34). He went out and wept bitterly *(eklausen pikrōs)*. Luke adds that the Lord turned and looked upon Peter (Luke 22:61). It was that look which brought Peter back to his senses. The aorist here does not emphasize, as Mark's imperfect does, the continued weeping. Tradition has it that all his life thereafter Peter could never hear a rooster crow without falling on his knees and weeping.

Doctrinal study. Law: Boasting results in embarrassment. Pride goes before the fall. Lame denial of what others know to be true. Cowardice that disavows the Lord. Loss of self-control that leads a person to resort to anything to save his own skin.

Gospel: Jesus understands threatening circumstances because He endured them Himself. He maintains control even in the most trying circumstances. Jesus is concerned about us when we lose control. Jesus still cares about us. He wants to keep us strong through our relationship with Him.

Parallel passages. The gospel parallels are Mark 16:62-72; Luke 22:56-62; John 18:15-18, 25-27. Other parallels are Matt. 26:35; Luke 22:31, 61; Rom. 7:24-25; 8:2; 14:13; 2 Cor. 3:5; Gal. 2:20b-21; Col. 1:27b; James 4:11-12.

Central thought. Peter's loss of self-control contrasts sharply to the self-control of Christ who, though threatened, showed loving concern for Peter.

Homiletical Treatment

Goal-malady-means approach. The goal is that the hearers will let the Holy Spirit manage their impulses and emotions rather than be managed by them. The malady is that too often the sinful self takes over and runs the show. The means to the goal is that Christ gives us a new self by which we can hold in check our evil desires.

Sermon outline. Introduction: Peter never thought it would happen to him. Only a few hours before he had said he would never deny Christ (Matt 26:35). And here he was, denying. Not just lying about his connection with Christ but firming up the lie with curses and oaths. What a sad loss of self-control! Yet it was perhaps understandable in the circumstances. He could have been arrested just for having associated with Jesus. He could have been sentenced to die along with Jesus. He was probably taken aback when the maid so suddenly and unexpectedly confronted him, and fear made him panic.

Fear can cause people to lose control of themselves and to do things they would never do otherwise. Like the man who, when the Titanic was sinking, disguised himself as a woman in order to get into one of the remaining lifeboats, or like the student who for fear of flunking out of school cheated in an exam.

The real reason, though, for loss of self-control is not so much fear as unchecked bodily desire. A person loses control of himself when he does not keep in check the hungers of the body for food, drink, comfort, reputation, work, or play. Part of the Spirit's task is to hold these appetites in check.

THE FRUIT OF THE SPIRIT IS SELF-CONTROL

I. Without the Spirit, self-control would be impossible.

    A. We all have a sinful self.

    B. The sinful self is powerful (Rom. 7:18-20, 23).

II. Self-control is possible because we have a new self under the control of Christ.

    A. Christ exercised complete control over Himself and His circumstances to atone for our failures.

    B. Christ stands ready to help us control ourselves.

Conclusion: We don't have to be managed by our impulses and emotions. We can manage them because the fruit of the Spirit is self-control.

Thematic approach. Peter's repeated denial is restated positively as an affirmation of the actual relationship of Peter and of us to Christ.

Sermon outline. Introduction: Twice Peter said: "I do not know the man." Peter had been with Jesus almost three years and had confessed Him to be the Christ of God. He did know Jesus. So do we.

WE KNOW JESUS OF NAZARETH

I. We know Jesus of Nazareth as One who sees our weakness.

    A. At times we, like Peter, think we are so strong we will never deny Christ (Matt. 26:33, 35).

    B. Yet there are times when we deny Christ by our silence if not by our spoken words.

    C. Jesus sees through our sham and discerns our weakness. On our own we cannot muster the self-control necessary to give consistent evidence that we know Jesus.

II. We know Jesus of Nazareth as One whose love leads us to repentance.

    A. Although our denials of Jesus merit His wrath, Jesus showed His love for us by atoning for our denials.

    B. He continues to reveal His love by altering us to the temptations to deny Him that come to us continually.

    C. The love of Christ moves us not only to weep over our sins of denial but to trust in Him for forgiveness.

Conclusion: We know Jesus of Nazareth as One who sees our weakness and loves us still. His love empowers us to exercise self-control so that we deny not Christ but ourselves.

Textual-topical approach. Peter's loss of control prompts a treatment of the topic of self-control that utilizes insights from the context as well as from the text but that otherwise moves independently of the text.

Sermon outline. Introduction: The greatest struggle most of us have is to control our desire for food, alcohol, approval, power, position. What happened to Peter is an inducement for us to

MAINTAIN SELF-CONTROL

I. We maintain self-control by becoming aware of threats to self-control.

    A. Reliance on one's own power (Matt. 25:33, 35)

B. Confidence in physical force (Matt. 26:51-52)

C. Careless association with enemies of Christ (Matt. 26:69)

II. We maintain self-control by utilizing helps to self-control.

A. Admitting the reality of sin in our lives

B. Sorrowing over our sin

C. Believing in Christ as the One who forgives our sin

Conclusion: Even though the flesh distorts our thinking and befuddles our common sense, the new self in Christ is stronger than instinctual drives and sinful patterns of thinking. Self-control is restored as this new self takes over.

Sermon Illustrations

The Spirit's fruit does not come from a graft that changes only the branches of our lives. Rather, fruit produced in our lives grows from roots planted deeply in the new life in Christ. The Spirit takes the control of our "self" away from Satan and restores it to us.

When our "self" is controlled by the new life in Christ, God can count on us to be back in self-control again. (Eldon Weisheit, "The Fruit of the Spirit Is Self-control," *The Lutheran Witness,* January 27, 1974, p. 5)

Other hands—cold and clammy ones—fumble for the controls of the inner self and seek to disengage the hand of the Spirit. Around Christian people are many for whom the swine are symbols of life. By and by even some Christians could imagine that it is a jolly thing to be a bit swinish. (Richard R. Caemmerer, "The Fruit of the Spirit Is Temperance" *The Lutheran Witness,* November 11, 1952, p. 3)

For there is no doubt about it: the flesh rains those blows upon us. Whether the craving be for drink or self-esteem or money or leisure, the blows come pounding in. They hit the brain as well as the body; they distort our thinking as well as our doing; they befuddle our plans and our common sense and, worst of all, our vision of God, who wants us to serve him with our entire selves and gave Jesus to die for us so that we might be freed from the bondage of the flesh. (Caemmerer, p. 3)

When we are convinced we are right we ought to ask God not to give us the victory, but to grant us self-control—control over our arrogance, our pride, our very assurance of rightness. (Guder, p. 126)

Self-control is never so needed as when we are right. When we are right it is fatally easy to excuse temper on the basis that we have been sorely tried by those in error; to excuse gossiping and discussing others maliciously on the basis that they are wrong and ought to be circumvented; to excuse being manipulative on the basis that we are only doing the Lord's work. (Guder, p. 127)

Today we see a new phenomenon in the Christian world—Christians who, on the basis that God loves us and wants us to be happy, make no attempt to curb their desires, however inexcusable their behavior. (Guder, p. 127)

A man and his wife were riding together on a horse along a dangerous road. At a very narrow place the wife became frightened and seized the rein nearest to her. Her husband quietly passed the other rein over to her and let go. Then she was more frightened than ever and said, "Oh, don't you let go!" He answered, "Two people cannot guide one horse; either I must drive it or you must." Then she gave him the reins and he drove safely past the danger. If we wish God to rule over us we must give all that we have into his hands and let him manage for us. If we don't let him take control, self will rule our lives. (From *Anecdotes and Illustrations*, by Wilbur E. Nelson, p. 75. Copyright 1971 by Baker Book House and used by permission)

Lent 6

Peace in Light of Matt. 27:11-24

Word Study of Peace

Usage in secular Greek. Eirēnē does not primarily denote a relationship between several people or an attitude, but a state. A state of peace was originally conceived of purely as an interlude in the everlasting state of war, but a state, nevertheless, from which flow all blessings for both land and people.

Eirēnē can sometimes signify a peaceful attitude, but even then the reference is more to the absence of hostile feelings than to the presence of kindly feelings to others. Thus it is seldom used for concord between men.

Old Testament usage. At root the Old Testament term usually translated "peace" means well-being with a strong emphasis on the material side. In many instances the word signifies bodily health or well-being and the related satisfaction. More commonly the term refers to a group, that is, to a nation enjoying prosperity.

The term occurs also when there is reference to a covenant. The relationship of peace is sealed by both parties in a covenant, or conversely, the covenant inaugurates a relationship of peace. Ezekiel says that God makes a covenant for Israel, and the context makes it clear that the relationship of peace is the result (Ezek. 34:25).

Although there is a basic material element in the Hebrew term, it is essentially a religious term when it is used in its full compass. Peace comes only and all sufficiently from God. This is strikingly expressed in Ps. 85:8-10 and Num. 6:26.

Peace in an earthly, political sense was never perfectly realized. After the Babylonian Captivity peace in a new and larger sense, a spiritual one, became one of the most important elements in the preaching of the prophets. Thus Jeremiah can write to the exiles that the Lord has for them plans for welfare and not for evil (Jer. 29:11). The term is given a spiritual sense also in Is. 48:18.

In a number of Old Testament passages peace is linked with eschatological expectation of a final state of eternal peace. When we have prophecy of a restoration of the conditions of Paradise (Is. 11:1f.) or expectation of a humble king in the last age who will bring in a time of peace (Zech. 9:9f.), even though the Hebrew term is not always used, we have a prophetic promise of peace in its widest possible import.

There is no specific Old Testament text that denotes peace as a specifically spiritual attitude of inward peace. Generally the Hebrew term clearly denotes something that may be seen, and thus it is emphatically a social concept.

New Testament usage. In the New Testament three conceptions of *eirēnē* are evident. First, peace is referred to as a feeling of peace and rest. To the confusion caused by prophecy at Corinth, Paul opposes peace as the normal state of things (1 Cor. 14:33).

The second New Testament conception is that of peace as the eschatological salvation of the whole man. The expected salvation is referred to in the Song of Zacharias (Luke 1:79) and in Luke 2:14. The reference is not so much to peace among men or with God but to the salvation which has come to earth.

The eschatological meaning of peace is seen especially in Rom. 8:6, where life and death are modes of existence that will be revealed as such eschatologically. So peace is the state of final fulfillment, the normal state of the new creation. Similarly in 2 Peter 3:14 peace suggests the perfect well-being associated with the restitution of Christians after the image of God. When Paul in his closing greetings often speaks of the God of peace, the designation is firmly linked with what Paul expects of the God of peace. It does not refer to the peace of soul, which is the result of grace, but to the salvation of man which comes from God.

A third and much less frequent conception of peace in the New Testament is that of peace as a state of reconciliation with God. The main passage here is Eph. 2:14-17. Peace thus means peace with God and within humanity. It denotes the healing of the enmity between Jews and Gentiles and also that of man toward God. In Rom. 5:1 and in Rom 5:10 the reference is to a relationship with God, a relationship in which the believer is placed toward God.

Once men have come into a state of reconciliation with God, they are urged to live at peace with one another. Passages such as Matt. 5:9; Eph. 4:3; 2 Tim. 2:22; James 3:18; 1 Peter 3:11 refer to concord among men.

Text Study of Matt. 27:11-24

General setting of text. This has already been commented on sufficiently.

Immediate context. The account of Jesus before Pilate is introduced by the first two verses of chapter 27. Between verses 2 and 11 Matthew has the description of Judas's remorse, his return of the ransom money, and his subsequent suicide. It is likely that this incident occurred chronologically just where Matthew has it, that is, after Jesus had been brought before Pilate but before Pilate had imposed the death sentence upon Jesus.

In the verse immediately following the text (v. 25) the people, instigated by their leaders, respond to Pilate with a terrible imprecation, the consequences of which they experienced in the destruction of Jerusalem and the dispersion which followed it.

Text in vernacular. V. 19. "Have nothing to do with that righteous man, for I have suffered much over Him today in a dream" (RSV). "Don't have anything to do with that good man! I had terrible dreams about Him last night" (Phillips). "Have nothing to do with that innocent man; I was much troubled on His account in my dreams last night" (NEB). "Have nothing to do with that righteous Man; for last night I suffered greatly in a dream because of Him" (NAS). There are no significant variations among the English translations.

Text in original. V. 11. *Tou hēgemonos* was technically an officer of the emperor, more exactly a procurator, a ruler under the emperor of a less important province and thus less important than a propraeter (as over Syria). Pilate represented Roman law. Therefore the question "Are you the king of the Jews?" is what really mattered. Pilate himself could be accused to Caesar for disloyalty. There were many rivals or pretenders in the empire. By His answer, *"su legeis,"* Jesus confesses that He is a king. But just what sort of a king did He claim to be? Pilate had a problem on his hands.

V. 13. Pilate apparently did not believe that this dignified, meek, inoffensive man was guilty of sedition, and he wanted to hear His defense, which he was willing to receive favorably. Pilate from the first showed reluctance to proceed with the trial, for he was not satisfied with the vague accusation that Jesus was a malefactor. But he could make nothing significant of Jesus' kingship either.

V. 14. Here the Greek is very precise, with a double negative. "He did not reply to him up to not even one word." The silent dignity of Jesus amazed Pilate, and he was strangely impressed.

V. 17. Pilate was clutching at every straw, seeking any loophole to escape condemning a harmless lunatic or exponent of a superstitious cult such as he deemed Jesus to be, certainly in no political sense a rival of Caesar. So he thought of the time-honored custom at the Passover of releasing a prisoner whom the people wished. For some reason Barabbas was a popular hero of sorts, leader of an insurrection or revolution, probably against Rome, and so guilty of the very crime they tried to fasten on Jesus. These two prisoners represented the antagonistic forces of all time.

V. 18. This seemed like an excellent expedient because Pilate knew the motives that led the leaders of the Sanhedrin to desire Christ's death. He knew they were jealous of Christ and saw that their accusation of Christ as a leader of sedition was nothing but a flimsy pretense.

V. 19. Just when Pilate was trying to enlist the people in behalf of Jesus, his wife sent a message about her dream. She called Jesus "that righteous man." Her sufferings must have increased Pilate's fears and unnerved him.

V. 22. Pilate must have been disappointed and indignant when the rabble asked for Barabbas. But he still had some hope of a better feeling in the crowd which would allow him to acquit Jesus. He did not dare to ask boldly as his conscience and the justice of the case dictated. If the popular voice was not with him, he would take no open step. He shirked his own responsibility and tried to hide his weakness and injustice behind popular clamor and prejudice.

V. 23. The particle *gar* implies a certain reasoning in the question, as if he were demanding from the people the ground of their decision. He descended to the level of arguing with a mob inflamed with passion for the blood of Jesus. This was a feeble protest by a flickering conscience. But this exhibition of weakness made the mob think that Pilate would not proceed. So they kept crying exceedingly (imperfect tense of repeated action). "It was like a gladiatorial show with all thumbs turned down."

V. 24. Nothing he did altered the determination of the crowd. There were ominous signs of a riot which would have to be suppressed, even at the sacrifice of principle and equity. Pilate submits to the popular will but tries to absolve his guilt by a symbolical action that would appeal to the Jewish sentiment. He acted as if the administration of justice lay with them and not with him. Pilate can wash his hands, but he cannot purify his heart and conscience. The washing of the hands was a mode of asserting innocence prescribed in the Mosaic law (Deut. 21:6; Ps. 26:6).

Doctrinal study. Law: In their pride the Jewish leaders could not brook Christ's threat to their authority. They resented Christ's popularity and in their bitter envy determined to get rid of Him. They knew very well that the truth was not on their side.

Pilate's question with its emphasis on the "you" is derisive and sarcastic. He displays the contemptuousness of cynical unbelief.

By placing Barabbas side by side with Jesus he treats Jesus as if He were guilty. Thereby he makes a concession to Christ's enemies. The result is to be expected. If sin is given a finger, it will soon take the whole hand.

His washing of his hands is evidence of the unrest in his heart. The mob had noticed his irresoluteness and cowardice and made the most of his weakness. This was Pilate's vulnerable point. He feared the emperor more than the gods and his conscience. He chose a cowardly way to pacify his conscience. He had made his choice. He had rejected the Savior.

Gospel: Jesus' bold confession before Pilate affirms His spiritual kingship. Christ's composure reveals a peace rooted in obedience to His Father's will.

Christ had done no evil. He put up with the evil of men to secure for them forgiveness and reconciliation with God. With the hostility between God and man broken down, there can be peace between man and God.

There can also be peace in one's own soul. There is no need to take desperate measures to pacify one's conscience.

It is not necessary to strive against other human beings as Pilate did with the Jewish leaders and with the mob. Christ makes possible a state of affairs in which people can be at peace with one another.

Parallel passages. Gospel parallels are Mark 15:2-19; Luke 23:2-25; and John 18:29—19:16a. It is obvious that Matthew omits many details which the other evangelists, and especially John, supply. Matthew evidently wished to stress Israel's guilt through its chosen leadership. Thus he emphasizes Pilate's reluctance in passing the final judgment, how he was influenced by his wife, and how the people might have been led if it had not been for their leaders. Other parallel passages are Is. 9:6; 26:3; 53:7; Jer. 6:14; 8:15; Luke 1:79; John 14:27; 19:9-11; Acts 3:14; 10:36; Rom. 5:1; Eph. 2:14; Col. 3:15; 1 Tim. 6:13.

Central thought. Peace with one's self and others depends on a relationship to the Prince of Peace.

Homiletical Treatment

Goal-malady-means approach. The goal is that the hearers will let the peace they have received from Christ make a greater impact on their personalities and human relationships. The malady is that we sometimes persist in conflict which gives little evidence of the peace we have and that we should practice. The means to the goal is that Christ procured for us a peace with God that enables us to live at peace with ourselves and with others.

Sermon outline. Introduction: The fruit of the Spirit is peace. But where is that peace? There is unrest in the world, in our nation, and in us. We worry about our health, our job, our debts, our children's future. How we long for peace in the world, in our nation, and in ourselves!

How shall we find the still point in a turning world, the center that gives meaning to all our restless activities? Shall we find it in tranquilizers, alcohol, self-help booklets?

Peace is not something we achieve, or attain, or even a quality within us. Peace is a state of being that is a gift of God to us.

PEACE IS A FRUIT OF THE SPIRIT

I. Peace is the state in which we are reconciled to God.
   A. Sin causes people to be at war with God.
   B. God made peace in Jesus Christ.
II. Peace is the state in which we are reconciled to ourselves.
   A. It is often most difficult to accept one's self.
   B. We can begin to be at peace with ourselves when we know we are at peace with God.
III. Peace is the state in which we are reconciled to others.
   A. We can do battle on the front of interpersonal relationships because we don't have to waste time doing battle with ourselves.
   B. Peace is not merely the absence of strife between people but the healing of old wounds and the transforming of relationships.

Conclusion: The struggle may ruffle us a bit at times. But peace is deeper than the surface of life and always is there. For peace is a fruit of the Spirit, even when we are a bit ragged around the edges.

Thematic approach. A theme deduced from the text addresses us in our unrest and offers the possibility of genuine peace.

Sermon outline. Introduction: World events and individual lives give evidence of unrest. At times we experience restlessness to the point where we wonder whether any real peace is possible. The text indicates

THE WAY TO PEACE

I. The way to peace is through admission of guilt.
   A. The crowd shouting, "Let Him be crucified," did not feel guilty about what they were doing.
   B. As long as people refuse to acknowledge their guilt on account of the

evil that is in them and that they perpetrate, they will not have peace.

 C. Admission of guilt is the way to peace, for such admission frees us from pretending we are better than we really are.

II. The way to peace is through reliance on Christ.

 A. Pilate felt guilty and vainly attempted to absolve himself.

 B. Nothing we do—weeping, praying, giving for charitable causes—can remove our guilt.

 C. Only Christ's blood, in the scourging and the crucifixion, can cleanse us from sin, remove our guilt, and give us peace.

III. The way to peace is through concern for others.

 A. Many, like Barabbas, live self-centered lives that lack peace.

 B. When, through faith in Christ, we have peace with God, we can be at peace with ourselves and seek to live in peace with others.

 C. We can utilize the power of our baptism to move beyond our own immediate problems. Peace is experienced as we help others to live in peace.

Conclusion: Unlike the crowd, we can admit our guilt. Unlike Pilate, we can find in Christ deliverance from guilt. Unlike Barabbas, we can become concerned about others. That is the way to peace in a world of unrest.

Textual-topical approach. The irony in a key word of the text becomes a handle for Gospel proclamation.

Sermon outline. Introduction: Pilate's wife warned her husband to have nothing to do with Jesus. Because of her dream she was sure Jesus was a righteous man who had done nothing deserving death. But Pilate's wife said much more than she realized.

JESUS IS INDEED A RIGHTEOUS MAN

 I. He was perfectly righteous; no one could accuse Him of sin. He also possessed a peace, evident in His conduct before Pilate, that came from walking in obedience to God's commands.

 II. Not only did He fulfil God's righteous demands with regard to keeping the Law but also God's righteous demand regarding the punishment for sin. By enduring that punishment on the cross Jesus broke down the hostility between God and people, making peace.

III. Not our righteousness but the perfect righteousness of Jesus is acceptable to God. It is reassuring to know that what Jesus did in His life, death, and resurrection He did for us.

IV. Through faith in Jesus we receive His righteousness in exchange for our sin. Clothed in Christ's righteousness, we are at peace with God.

Conclusion: Pilate's wife said: "Have nothing to do with that righteous man." From our perspective, to have nothing to do with Jesus is to reject Him by saying we don't need Him or by pretending to believe Him. But we have much to do with Jesus. Daily we trust in Him for righteousness; daily we receive His peace; by our life we daily honor Him as our Savior and Lord.

Sermon Illustrations

Anyone who offers a quick solution to the questions of world peace, racial tensions, social disorders, or disturbed minds and consciences is a quack. Solutions to major problems in society have always been worked out with blood and sweat and tears, and if we find some short-cut to give us complete personal happiness and serenity in the midst of the agony of others, we have reached a phony peace. When the cry of the world's suffering reaches me I don't want to be offered an earplug. When the threat of disaster looms up black I don't want rose-tinted glasses. And if my own disquiet is caused by some wrong I'm doing to others, I don't want to compound that wrong by drugging my conscience into a blissful detachment. There is a dimension here—in suffering and in evil—that cannot be penetrated by any surface therapy, or reached by any lightning cure. The prophet Jeremiah had something to say about this phony peace: "For they have healed the hurt of the daughter of my people slightly, saying, Peace, peace; when there is no peace." (David H. C. Read, *I Am Persuaded* [New York: Charles Scribner's Sons, 1961] pp. 112—113)

The calm (of Jesus) was only to be found in a mind set like a flint to do the Father's will, and a conscience clear as the noonday sun. This peace is not an escape-hatch through which we slip away, it is the by-product of a decision to do, here at the danger point, what we know within us to be right. (Read, p. 116)

There were times when I made myself miserable because my husband and I were having a financial struggle and doing without the new furniture and clothes I longed for; and when a friend invited us over to see the house they had just built, my envy was like a pain within me. I arrived home after that in such an angry depression that I was almost ill. The daydreams in which I indulged, dreams of a sudden huge inheritance, an unexpected legacy, made me more discontented than ever. The peace which is given by God did nothing for me, not because it was not there, but because I was indulging in emotions which squashed peace in its infancy. (Guder, p. 52)

It would be nice if that one battle had been the end of it—if I could report that since that struggle ended I had been in a state of tranquility, with no struggles, no battles to fight, and no wounds sustained. But we are not such simple creatures as all that. There were other battles to be fought, and there are present and future battles to be fought. The peace that belongs to the Christian is not the peace of inactivity, but the peace of one whose decision is made and who is on his way. (Guder, pp. 53-54)

We may in our eagerness to keep everything peaceful...simply sweep all disagreements under the rug and pretend they are not there. When that happens, a cosmetic, purely superficial unity has been maintained at the cost of honesty. No one expresses his real feelings because to do so might ruffle the surface of that veneer of harmony. But genuine relationships cannot exist where there is no honesty. (Guder, p. 57)

If the patron saint of Ireland is St. Patrick and the patron saint of England is St. George, then the patron saint of America must be St. Vitus. (Norman Vincent Peale)

...in the thousands of years of recorded history there have been more than 8,000 peace treaties and only a few dozen years of actual peace. (G. E. Nitz, "The Fruit of the Spirit Is Peace," *The Lutheran Witness,* August 19, 1952, p. 3)

A huge concrete peace arch is in the town of Blaine, Wash., on the boundary between the United States and Canada, symbolizes a peace which for decades has existed between these two great nations. But the Cross of Christ is the greatest peace monument ever erected. From this Cross God's peace is proclaimed to all the world, and through the Spirit and the Word this peace is created in the heart of every true believer. (Nitz, p. 3)

It's a cop-out peace
    that avoids problems of life.
It's going to the mountains
    when violence is in the city.
It's shutting one's eyes
    to injustice
    to hunger
    to prejudice
    to fear.
It's passing by on the other side.
It's using drugs and booze
   busyness and
   religion
      to avoid one's own conflicts.
But it is not peace.

Some see peace as winning.
    To the victor belongs the spoils.
    Might makes right.
    We won the peace
      because you lost the war.
It's peace decreed by authority,
    peace that makes you
    think as I think
    like as I like
    hate what I hate,
    and do what I do.
It's peace enforced by
    guns and bombs
    walls and bars
    laws and judgments.
But it is not peace.

But there is peace—real peace.
. . . .
It is not peace with honor
    but peace by grace.
It is not peace at any price

but peace bought by paying
the wages of sin.
It is not peace that is earned
but peace that is given.

(Eldon Weisheit, "The Fruit of the Spirit
Is Peace," *The Lutheran Witness,*
November 18, 1973, p. 15)

Kindness in Light of Matt. 26:26-29

Word Study of Kindness

Usage in secular Greek. Chrēstotēs is used to characterize persons as having honesty, respectability, or worthiness. It can also mean kindness, friendliness, mildness, whether publicly or privately.

Old Testament usage. In passages like Gen. 20:13 and Gen. 40:14 the Hebrew term translated "kindness" refers specifically to the kindness of human beings toward one another. But in most of the Old Testament passages in which the Hebrew term is used, the reference is to God's kindly disposition or mode of action. All of the English translations with the exception of the KJV and Beck thus translate the Hebrew term as "steadfast love" or "constant love" rather than "kindness."

New Testament usage. Chrēstotēs is used of God only in the Pauline writings, where it denotes God's gracious attitude and act toward sinners. In Titus 3:4 *chrēstotēs* is elucidated by the description of the fullness of the salvation that has come in Christ, including the eschatological consummation. That consummation, depicted as a rising again and a ruling with Christ in the heavenly world, is the content of *chrēstotēs* in Eph. 2:7. Thus *chrēstotēs* expressed the comprehensive fullness of Christian salvation. The designation of God's saving work in Christ as kindness implies that by this work in and through Christ God is manifested according to His true nature.

Paul, however, also uses *chrēstotēs* as expressing the great experience that God's love, which is revealed in Christ and shed abroad in the hearts of His people by the Spirit, works itself out in them as kindness toward their neighbors. Thus, not only in Gal. 5:22 but also in 2 Cor. 6:6 and Col. 3:12 kindness has far more than general humanitarian content.

Text Study of Matt. 26:26-29

General setting of text. This has already been commented on.

Immediate context. The verses immediately preceding the text (20-25) contain Jesus' identification of Judas as the traitor. Not only Matthew but also Mark and John emphasize that the identification of Judas as the betrayer took place during the Passover meal that preceded the institution of the Sacrament (Matt. 26:23; Mark 14:20; John 13:26). From John's account it appears that Judas left before the words of institution were spoken. The verses immediately following the text (30f.) tell of Jesus leaving the Upper Room and going to the Mount of Olives, to Gethesemane, where His suffering begins. Between the conclusion of the Lord's Supper and the departure to the Mount of Olives Jesus delivered His farewell address to His disciples (John 14:1—16:33) and also His sacerdotal prayer (John 17:1-26).

Text in vernacular. V. 28. "...My blood of the new testament..." (KJV). "...the blood of the new agreement..." (Phillips). "...My blood, which seals God's covenant..." (TEV). All the other English versions use the word *covenant.* There are no other significant variations in the English translations.

Text in original. V. 26. The Greek *touto* (this) is the neuter and therefore not in agreement with bread *(artos),* which is masculine. It can be explained, however, as "This which I give you, this which you receive." There is no room here for metaphor or figure. He is not figuratively describing Himself, His office, or His work, as when He calls Himself the Good Shepherd, the Door, the Vine, the Way. Obviously the disciples could not understand this sentence; they could only believe. This was not just a commemorative rite, not simply a way of remembering Christ's death and suffering. Now, in this rite, the bread would serve as a means of bringing to the eater Christ's body and with it a great blessing.

V. 27. The word *all (pantes)* makes it clear that all who partake of this supper are to receive both the bread and the wine.

V. 28. The covenant *(tēs diathēkēs)* harks back to the covenant God made with Israel. The covenant was God's, not Israel's, although the covenant obligated Israel, and Israel assumed those obligations. Another possible English translation of the Greek word is "will" or "testament." A will and testament emanates only from the testator. Christ brought the fulfilment of the promises God had made to Israel in the Old Testament covenant. Thus the word *testament* indicates that God gives to us the blessings Christ has brought. Both the Old Testament "covenant" and the New Testament "testament" were connected with blood. The Old Testament covenant was sealed with the blood of animal sacrifice, as is evident from Ex. 24:4-8. This blood promised, pointed to, the blood of Christ that would seal the new testament by which we inherit all that His blood purchased for us. The old covenant could be written in animal blood because it consisted of promise; the new testament would be written in the blood of the Son of God because it conveyed the fulfilment of the promise. The preposition *peri,* in the Greek connected with "many," indicates the persons involved, and the preposition *eis,* connected with forgiveness, indicates the purpose or effect upon these persons. The absence of the articles in the Greek stresses the nouns, remission and sins, the sending away or complete removal of sin whereby we miss the mark.

V. 29. The *oumē* (by no means) is a strong negative. The expression "until that day" refers to the time when the disciples will be drinking with Christ new *(kainon)* in the heavenly kingdom. Here note Rev. 19:9. From Luke 22:16 we conclude that the heavenly feast will be a heavenly fulfilment of the Lord's Supper. The wine is to be understood as a symbol of the pleasure of the heavenly feast that is new in contrast to that which has taken place on earth. Jesus is saying that He will die but that the day is coming when He will be drinking a wonderful new wine with His disciples in heaven.

Doctrinal study. The Lord's Supper is the New Testament passover. Jesus opens the new era in which the Paschal Lamb is eaten. The Lord's Supper is a feast and not a sacrifice, a feast in which the offering is eaten. At this supper the Lord is the host. The Lord's Supper is not merely a commemoration but a feast of union with the Lord and a communion with the other participants (1 Cor. 10:27). Jesus "gave thanks" for the bread and the wine as vehicles for the nourishment and strengthening of the spiritual life. With this blessing He consecrates the bread and wine for a new and holy purpose in the Sacrament. They are now divorced from their usual purpose and are to be bearers of the body and blood of the Lord. The bread and wine do not change into the body and blood of Christ.

This is the last will and testament of Jesus. Among men it is the duty of a testator to use plain and simple words, avoiding terms that are misleading. The beneficiary has the right and also the duty to abide by the literal interpretation.

When we receive and eat the bread, we receive and eat Christ's body; when we receive and drink the wine, we receive and drink Christ's blood. Both bread and wine and body and blood are really present. This is a deep mystery.

This text is pure Gospel. The Law is implied, however, in verse 28, where it is made clear that our sins were the cause of Christ having to pour out His blood on the cross. The Law can be deduced also from verse 29. As long as we are on this earth, we have reason to continue to partake of the Lord's Supper because of the need of forgiveness and of strength before we reach the new and perfect fulfilment of the Sacrament at the marriage feast of the Lamb.

Parallel passages. Parallel accounts are Mark 14:22-25; Luke 22:17-20; 1 Cor. 11:23-25. Other parallels are Luke 6:35; 1 Cor. 10:16-17; 11:26-29; Eph. 4:32; Heb. 8:8-12.

Central thought. Jesus showed kindness to His own by giving them His body and His blood for the forgiveness of their sins.

Homiletical Treatment

Goal-malady-means approach. The goal is that the hearers will partake frequently of Christ's body and blood for strength to practice kindness. The malady is that we sometimes forget that the Lord's Supper, by bringing to us Christ's kindness in His forgiveness, enables us to be kind. The means to the goal is the kindness Christ shows us in the Sacrament of His body and blood.

Sermon outline. Introduction: How remarkable that when Satan was marshalling his forces, when Judas had made his contract to betray the Son of God, when the soldiers and the guards stood ready to follow the traitor wherever he would lead them, when Caiaphas was drumming up a meeting of the Sanhedrin in anticipation of Christ's capture, Jesus, knowing all that would happen, had His disciples in His heart. On the night of His betrayal and the eve of His death, His concerns were for the disciples. He knew how frail and

52

frightened they were, what a jolt their faith would suffer, how His death would overwhelm them. So now He would show them kindness that would support and strengthen them.

That night Jesus did not single out only the disciples. He looked into the future and saw how we would need support and strength. That night Jesus showed kindness also to us.

THE SACRAMENT OF HIS BODY AND BLOOD
SHOWS JESUS' KINDNESS TO US—

I. His kindness in forgiving our sins.
   A. We need forgiveness.
   B. We can be sure of forgiveness.
II. His kindness in enabling us to live as the forgiven.
   A. Christ implanted His kindness in us.
   B. Christ demonstrates His kindness through us.
   C. Christ will perfect His kindness in us.

Thematic approach. The covenant concept of the text is made the theme of a sermon that explores the meaning of the covenant relationship in both the Old and New Testaments.

Sermon outline. Introduction: A covenant is an agreement initiated by two parties. The Bible speaks of a covenant between God and Christians, which covenant, however, is initiated entirely by God. The Lord's Supper is an expression of this covenant.

THE LORD'S SUPPER IS A COVENANT MEAL

I. The Lord's Supper is a covenant rooted in unmerited kindness.
   A. God chose undeserving Israel to be His people.
   B. God has made us part of the New Testament Israel.
   C. To convince us of His unmerited kindness, Christ unites us with Himself in the covenant meal.
II. The Lord's Supper is a covenant sealed by atoning blood.
   A. The blood of sacrificial animals pointed the Old Testament Israel to the atonement that made the covenant possible.
   B. The blood of Christ effected the cleansing from sin which makes it possible for us to be children of the convenant.
   C. To seal the covenant Christ gives us His body and blood in the covenant meal.
III. The Lord's Supper is a covenant anticipating heavenly glory.
   A. The Old Testament believers looked forward to a glorious restoration of their blighted hopes.
   B. We New Testament Christians see that restoration in Christ.
   C. In the covenant meal we look forward to the fulfilment of the covenant in glory.

Conclusion: The Lord's Supper assures us we are God's covenant people, made such by His kindness, cleansed daily by His blood, and looking forward to glory.

Doctrinal approach. With the term *kindness* being used to describe the benefits of the Lord's Supper, the sermon becomes a vehicle for presenting the doctrinal content of the text in a way that comforts and encourages the hearers.

Sermon outline. Introduction: When we Lutherans refer to God's Word, Baptism, and Holy Communion as means of grace, we're saying these are channels by which God brings us His grace or kindness. The text focuses on

THE LORD'S SUPPER AS A CHANNEL
OF CHRIST'S KINDNESS

I. It bestows Christ's kindness on us now.
   A. We receive the forgiveness Christ earned for us by His body and His blood.
   B. We receive strength to demonstrate Christ's kindness in our lives.
II. It points to Christ's kindness hereafter.
   A. Our partaking of the Lord's Supper reminds us that Christ's kindness works itself out in our final salvation.
   B. Our partaking of the Lord's Supper enables us to live with the hope that we shall one day partake of a heavenly banquet.

Conclusion: What a channel of divine kindness the Lord's Supper is! What a privilege to partake of it often!

Sermon Illustrations

Kindness does not operate well under a spotlight; it is fleeting and fast, shared with a smile, a word, a touch. Kindness is not rehearsed or premeditated; it happens because one has kindness to give, not because kindness is needed. (Eldon Weisheit, "The Fruit of the Spirit Is Kindness," *The Lutheran Witness,* January 6, 1974, p. 14)

...It was kindness that gave [Christ] the time to talk to small children, to touch a deaf man's ear, to spare a bridegroom embarrassment by providing wedding wine.
...It was kindness that made Him see beyond His own pain to the needs of a mother, a friend, a soldier, a thief.
...His kindness invited back one who had denied Him and extended pierced hands as evidence to one who had doubted Him." (Weisheit, "Kindness," p. 14)

The discourtesy shown by Christians is an act of violence toward the well-being and comfort of other persons, just as were the rock-throwing, obscenity-shouting, and rioting of the '60s. Even those of us who are not compulsive talkers are frequently guilty of the rudeness of not listening; interrupting when we want to speak. We do this especially with our children, a habit which makes nonsense of our admonitions to them to be polite and not interrupt when others are speaking. I know this so well because my own daughter pointed out to me just what I was doing. She was in high school at the time and one day, provoked by my constant interruptions, she said, "Mother, you never listen to me. You interrupt me all the time and never try and hear a word I say. I don't know why I bother to tell you anything, because you don't care." (Guder, pp. 81—82)

After I began doing some public speaking myself I realized even more how frustrating it is to concentrate on getting a message across while at the same time whispers are coming from somewhere in the audience. It is especially disconcerting to see, out of the corner of one's eye, two people giggling together. One thinks, "What did I say? Did I make a slip of the tongue? Have I said something ridiculous?" (Guder, pp. 82—83)

Kindness also produces tact—that is, the ability to smooth over awkward situations, to say or do the thing that will ease a tense situation or avert an unpleasant scene. If courtesy is the everyday coin of kindness, then tact is the gold. It is called for when courtesy has been unequal to the task of making everyone comfortable. (Guder, p. 83)

Good Friday

Love in Light of Mark 15:33-39

Word Study of Love

Usage in secular Greek. The meaning of *agapan* is variable. Often it means no more than "to be satisfied" with something. It can mean "to receive" or "to greet" or "to honor." Often it has the meaning of "to prefer," in the sense of esteeming one person more highly than another or setting one good or aim above another.

When interchanged with *eran* or *filein, agapan* is often a mere synonym which is set alongside the other two for the sake of emphasis or stylistic variation.

Old Testament usage. The picture changes completely in the Old Testament. The main word for love in the Hebrew text applies to the passionate love between man and woman, to the selfless loyalty of friendship, and to resolute adherence to righteousness. Thus the Hebrew word covers all of the three Greek terms, *agapan, filein,* and *eran.* However, the religious eroticism in the Greek *eros* is lacking in the Old Testament religion, distinguishing it sharply from the fertility cults of surrounding nations as well as from the Greek world. The love of God for Israel is not impulse but will (Deut. 7:13). The love for God and neighbor demanded of the Israelites (Deut. 6:5; Lev. 19:18) is not intoxication but act. In contrast to the Greek *eros,* the love extolled in the Old Testament is a jealous love that chooses one among thousands, holds him, and will allow no breach of loyalty.

New Testament usage. For Jesus, love for God is the great and basic demand (Matt. 22:39). To love God means to base one's whole being on God, to cling to Him with unreserved confidence, to leave with Him all care, to listen faithfully and obediently to His orders, to cut away all that hinders from serving God alone. In stressing love for one's neighbor, Jesus does not give a list of the various classes of men, from those who are nearest to those who are farthest away, but He shows that whoever stands closest to the man in need has a neighborly duty toward him. He fulfils his neighborly duty whose heart detects the distress of the other and who simply does what has to be done and what he can do.

In His demand to love one's enemies (Matt. 5:43f.; Luke 6:32f.) Jesus opposed the Jewish tradition. The love of enemies that Jesus demands is the attitude of the new people of God. They are to show love without expecting it to be returned. They should do good to those who hate them and pray for them (Matt. 5:44; Luke 6:27f).

Jesus can make such a demand without delusion or sentimentality because He proclaimed and created a new world situation. He proclaimed the mercy of God as an event that places man in a completely different situation. There is a new relationship of God to man that lays the foundation for a new relationship of man to man.

The new relationship of man to God made possible by God's forgiveness is effected by the death of Jesus, God's "beloved" Son (Matt. 12:18). The Son brings the remission of sins to which man replies with grateful love and to which he should respond with an unconditional readiness to help and forgive his fellows.

God has the first word. He establishes the relationship. From Him proceeds everything that may be called *agapē*. Our decision to love is possible because God creates for us the life which first makes us men of will and action in the true sense. God awakens in man the faith in which he is wholly referred to God. But faith comes into action and finds true actualization only through love (Gal. 5:6). God pours forth the Spirit into His believers (Rom. 5:5), and the Spirit liberates man for supreme activity in love. We are capable of active love toward God and man only to the extent that we are passive before God (Phil. 3:12).

The goal of our love is not only to love God but our neighbor (Gal. 5:13). For Paul, neighborly love is essentially brotherly (Gal. 6:10). It is service rendered to fellow-citizens as the new people of God. Brotherly love is a readiness for service and sacrifice, for forgiveness and consideration, for help and sympathy, for lifting up the fallen and restoring the broken (Rom. 12:9f.; 1 Cor. 13:4f.; Gal. 5:25f.).

In James faith acquires living force to the extent that it is active in love. The truth of faith working through love (Gal. 5:6) James translates into practical commands which prevent any comfortable escape (2:14; 5:1f.). In the first letter of John love is a vital movement, a form of existence, an actualization of God in this world (1 John 4:7, 19).

Text Study of Mark 15:33-39

General setting of text. Mark's gospel is mainly narrative, and the style is direct and simple. Early writers agree that Mark was the interpreter for Simon Peter with whom he was at one time, according to Peter's own statement, in Babylon (Rome) (1 Peter 5:13). The gospel is full of details that apparently came from Peter's discourses which Mark heard. Mark wrote mainly for Gentile readers, for he seldom refers to the Old Testament. His gospel is the shortest of the four.

Immediate context. The immediately preceding verses (29-32) tell of the derision heaped upon Christ by passers-by as He hung on the cross. We are told also in verse 32b that the thieves crucified with Him reviled Him.

The verses immediately following (40-41) name some of the many faithful women who had ministered to Jesus while He was living and who now stood at some distance from the cross observing His death.

Text in vernacular. Except for verse 39 where Phillips and the NEB have "a Son of God" rather than "the Son of God," as in all the other translations, there is no significant variation in the translations.

Text in original. V. 33. The word *holēn* in connection with land, the "whole" land or earth, indicates that not just the Jewish land and certainly not just Jerusalem and its vicinity, but a much wider area was covered by this darkness. The darkness was a miraculous act of God signifying judgment.

The words of Christ's cry are quoted from Ps. 22:1 in which David prophetically described the suffering and dying of the Messiah. During those three hours of darkness Jesus was made sin for us (2 Cor. 5:21), a curse for us (Gal. 3:13), and thus God turned completely away from Him. The world's sin and curse lying upon Him separate Him from the Father. No one can know the full meaning of God forsaking or abandoning Jesus. We can say that Jesus tasted God's wrath on account of sin, and only by His being actually forsaken could the full price for redemption be paid.

V. 35. Some of the bystanders mistook the opening words of Jesus' cry as a call to Elijah, probably because Elijah was believed to hold some relation to the Messiah as the one who would precede and introduce Him to the Jews.

V. 36. At this point John (19:28-29) has the word of Jesus, "I thirst." One, probably a soldier, ran to give Him the sponge soaked in sour wine. This soldier and the others nearby continued to mock Him.

V. 37. All the Synoptists mention the loud cry of Jesus. Such a cry was most unusual for one who was about to die by crucifixion. Here is indication that Jesus' death was voluntary in accordance with what He Himself had said (John 10:8). The word for dying that Mark uses is *exepneusen,* "to expire," meaning that He breathed out His spirit. His spirit was breathed out into His Father's hands (Luke 23:46).

V. 38. The veil rent at the Lord's death was the inner curtain that hung between the Holy Place and the Holy of Holies. This curtain was massive and richly embroidered. The rending announced that the ministrations of the Jewish high priest had come to an end because the great high priest Jesus by His atoning blood had entered the holy of holies of heaven. Now all people can come nigh through the blood of Christ, for heaven has been opened by His death.

V. 39. The centurion, the high ranking Roman officer probably in command of the detail that crucified Jesus, was impressed by the words and demeanor of Jesus on the cross. The fact that the article is left out of "Son of God" is not significant since the expression "Son of God" as used by Matthew and Mark is equivalent to a proper name. The centurion obtained this name from the Jews and no doubt used it in their sense. If he had intended to say only that Jesus was nothing more than a good human being, it does not seem likely that Matthew or Mark would have recorded what he said. What he said could also be translated, "This man was God's Son."

Doctrinal study. A mystery that God should be forsaken by God. Yet it was a real God-forsakenness. The second Adam was forced to experience the agonies and terrors of hell in order to free us from them.

Their giving Jesus vinegar to drink was in fulfilment of Ps. 69:21. The loud cry, "It is finished" (John 19:30), is the mighty voice of victory over Satan.

Jesus saying, "Father, into Thy hands I commend My spirit," indicates that He has again found His Father and now He dies with Scripture (Ps. 31:6) just as He was dead according to Scripture. With this word He summons death.

Here at the cross, God's love and justice meet without either one denying the other.

Parallel passages. Gospel parallels are Matt. 27:45-56 and Luke 23:44-49. Other possible parallel passages have already been cited in the word study and will not be repeated here.

Central thought. The central thought of the text is that God loved sinners so much that to save them He abandoned His own Son on the cross.

Homiletical Treatment

Goal-malady-means approach. The goal is that the hearers will let the love God showed in Christ become a reality in their lives. The malady is that we do not always love sacrificially and unconditionally. The means to the goal is the sacrificial and unconditional love God showed us in the death of His Son.

Sermon outline. Introduction: Love is the first fruit listed by Paul in Gal. 5:22. It is also the most important. We know very well that human beings need more than anything else to love and be loved. But when we see in the world and in our own lives so much hatred and selfishness, it does seem as though love is not a reality but only an ideal we approve of intellectually and agree with philosophically.

Why is love so desired and yet so denied? Why is it that that which should live in the heart has survived only in the mind? Perhaps it is because we have failed to understand that love is not a fruit of the mind but of the Spirit.

LOVE IS THE FRUIT OF THE SPIRIT

I. God gave love to us.

A. We did not deserve that love.

B. God gave His love to us in the death of His Son.

II. God produces love in us.

A. God's love grows in us when we believe the love God has for us in Christ.

B. The love God produces in us is action.

Conclusion:
> See, from his head, his hands, his feet,
> Sorrow and love flow mingled down.
> Did e'er such love and sorrow meet
> Or thorns compose so rich a crown?
>
> Were the whole realm of nature mine,
> That were a tribute far too small;
> Love so amazing, so divine,
> Demands my soul, my life, my all!

Thematic approach. The theme of the sermon focuses on the depths of God with which we are confronted in the death of Christ.

Sermon outline. Introduction: The unnatural darkness, the anguished lament, the loud cry before He died, the temple curtain tearing, all point to God's involvement in the death of Christ. We get a glimpse into the mystery of God.

THE CROSS LEADS US INTO THE DEPTHS OF GOD

I. We see God's terrible wrath against sin.
   A. Sin is not just a human weakness that God overlooks.
   B. The God-forsakenness of Jesus on the cross tells us that God hates sin and must punish it.
II. We see God's boundless love toward sinners.
   A. Jesus who had no sin took our sin upon Himself.
   B. God loved us sinners so much that He became a man and suffered sin's punishment for us.
III. We see His all-sufficient atonement for sinners' sin.
   A. The torn curtain in the temple signified that animals no longer needed to be sacrificed in atonement for sin.
   B. By the blood of His Son God made a once-and-for-all atonement for your sins and mine and for the sins of the whole world.

Conclusion: At the cross we see the depths of God's wrath, love, and atoning power. His wrath against sin is real, but so is His love for sinners. God's wrath and love met at the cross in such a way as to effect an all-sufficient atonement which assures us of God's love and kindles love in us.

Textual-topical approach. The symbolism conveyed by the torn curtain is developed with the aid of the text and of Hebrews 9:11-14.

Sermon outline. Introduction: The death of Christ is the supreme testimony of God's love for the world. Also many of the events that accompanied Christ's death speak powerfully of God's love. Such an event is the tearing of the temple curtain recorded by Mark and also by Matthew and Luke.

THE TORN CURTAIN ASSURES US OF GOD'S LOVE

I. It assures us of a love that secured our redemption.
   A. The complete tearing of the curtain between the Holy Place and the Holy of Holies symbolized the complete ending of the Old Testament system of priesthood and sacrifice.
   B. Christ's sacrificing of His sinless self for us makes all other atoning sacrifices unnecessary.
   C. Christ's blood provides a cleansing that makes us acceptable to the holy God.
   D. Christ has entered the holy of holies of heaven, which we too will one day enter by the blood of Jesus.
II. It assures us of a love that motivates our service to God.
   A. The tearing of the curtain signified that we no longer have to serve God by prescribed rituals and ceremonies but in a freedom dictated by love.

B. We serve not to make ourselves acceptable to God but to celebrate the fact that God has already accepted us in Christ.

C. We serve by confessing Christ to be the Son of God and our only Mediator with God.

D. With a conscience purified from dead works we serve in a faith that works by love.

Conclusion: The torn curtain in the temple assures us of the love of God which makes possible our new existence in Jesus Christ.

Sermon Illustrations

As we look through the window or page through the catalog and say, "I'd like that," we must remember that love is the fruit of the Spirit. We don't go out and buy love or order it by phone. It is a gift. (Eldon Weisheit, "The Fruit of the Spirit Is Love," *The Lutheran Witness,* October 7, 1973, p. 5)

Love fails in the bud when we see it as what others owe us rather than what we need to give to others. Love becomes plastic fruit when we talk about it but do not do it. Love rots when we give it on the basis of guilt or greed or manipulation. (Weisheit, "Love," p. 5)

Love, for most humans, is never unconditional. It hinges upon our being, or doing, what others want us to be or do... The list of those I must please grows longer and longer. Needing desperately to be loved, we try to meet the demands of those around us. But we, the victims, are also the persecutors because we impose our demands on others and, as they do, punish them when they don't meet our standards. (Guder, pp. 21—22)

Our obligation now was to live a perfect life the way the Bible described it and it was no wonder God was angry with us after he had done so much and our return was so poor. How did I get such an idea? How do so many of us acquire such a warped picture of the love of God? It seems to me that in spite of all the Bible verses and the teaching we get about the love of God and the forgiveness of God we believe what we experience more than what we are taught. And if we see love as conditional, if we don't experience forgiveness from our parents and those around us, we will naturally interpret all the Bible has to say about love in the light of our experience. Only the Holy Spirit can open our eyes to the love of God for us now, just as we are. (Guder, pp. 22—23)

That new look at God means that instead of seeing him as the angry old man—or the benevolent Santa Claus, only interested in making us happy—or the dispassionate Creator, far removed from his creation—we see him as he meant us to, in the person of Jesus Christ.... On that last night with his disciples Jesus said, "The man who has seen me has seen the Father." (Guder, p. 24)

[The dusty traveler] walked up the steps of a small, neatly kept farm house. "Hello, what do you want?" The stranger answered only with this question, "Does God live here?" The woman was startled. She thought she might have misunderstood. Once again she asked: "What is it that you want?" The tired-looking man's reply was the same: "Does God live here?" With that, the woman slammed the door shut in the visitor's face and ran to the back of the house to see her husband....

...He became incensed when he heard of the stranger's question. "Didn't you tell him we attend church without fail every Sunday?" "That wasn't what he asked, John," she replied; "he asked, 'Does God Live here?'" "Well, didn't you tell him we are heavy contributors and that you are active in the Guild, while I've been an elder for eight years?" "That wasn't what he asked, John. He asked 'Does God live here?'" So they talked the matter over. And finally they came to a conclusion. It was a sad one. They decided that God did not live there! (Deffner and Andersen, *For Example,* p. 142)

A farmer printed on his weather vane the words "God is love." Someone asked him if he meant to imply that the love of God was as fickle as the wind. The farmer answered, "No, I mean that whichever way the wind blows, God is love. If it blows cold from the north, or biting from the east, God is still love just as much as when the warm south or gentle west winds refresh our fields and flocks. God is always love." (Dennison, p. 129)

A minister called at the home of a family where the father took little interest in the church and seldom attended services. The minister hoped to persuade the man to join his wife in active membership, and carefully prepared what he had to say. Sure enough, the following Sunday the man came to church. But imagine the minister's surprise when a few weeks later the man told him, "It wasn't your argument that moved me. But remember when we were talking and little Jimmy came into the room? I was about to send him away, when you picked him up, patted him, and played a finger game with him. I thought to myself, Any man who loves little children must have something to say from the pulpit." (Dennison, pp. 132—33)

It is in many ways very reassuring to know when and where one can stop loving one's neighbor with good conscience. Generally, to know the answer to this question is of more interest and importance than the question of when and where we must begin to love our neighbor.

In the first place, it makes us feel more comfortable morally to be able to say: "Here I have really fulfilled my quota of love and forbearance. No more is required of me. Even God doesn't ask for more." It is the charm of all religions of law that they assign to a person a definite and limited quantum of obligations, of work, sacrifice, love, and decorum. And when a man has fulfilled his quota he is, so to speak, pensioned off and he can relax with a good conscience. (From *Christ and the Meaning of Life* by Helmut Thielicke, p. 73, © 1962 Harper & Row; reprint © 1975 by Baker Book House. Used by permission)

Joy in Light of John 20:11-18

Word Study of Joy

Usage in secular Greek. The noun *chara* means rejoicing, merriness. In Greek philosophy joy is an object of reflection and is barely distinguished from *hēdonē* (pleasure). Religiously, *chara* is a basic mood in mystery piety. Joy now appears as an eschatological concept in connection with the expectation of the world-savior. The emotional milieu of Jesus' birth thus has an echo in the pagan world.

Old Testament usage. In the Old Testament joy is not just inward. It has a cause and finds expression. It thus aims at sharing, especially as festal joy. It is a disposition of the whole man. This is the point when the heart is called its organ. Frequently God and His saving acts are occasions and objects of joy (Neh. 8:10; Ps. 5:11; 9:2; 32:11; Is. 35:10). The specific reason for joy is to be found in concrete demonstrations of salvation (Ex. 18:9; 1 Sam. 2:1). God's law is the object of joy in Ps. 119:16. God's word is the object of joy in Jer. 15:16. The Old Testament mentions also secular joy, as in Jer. 25:10 where God says that He will banish from them the voice of gladness...of the bridegroom and of the bride, and in Ps. 104:15 where the reference is to wine that makes glad the heart. Most common, though, is the festal joy of God's people ritually celebrated. Examples of such expressions of joy are Ps. 33 and Ps. 95.

The Old Testament usage of the term for joy culminates in eschatology (Is. 12:6; 25:9; Zech. 2:10). The roots of this joy are to be found in the connection between joy and kingship (Zech. 9:9).

New Testament usage. Among the Synoptists Luke puts the greatest accent on joy. The mood of joy dominant at the birth of Jesus (Luke 2:10) persists throughout the gospel as joy at the acts of Jesus (Luke 13:17; 19:6). Luke adds a final note when he says that the disciples returned to Jerusalem "with great joy" (Luke 24:52).

The thought of joy in suffering is stressed especially in 1 Peter. The general concept of suffering is given concrete shape as suffering for the faith (1 Peter 1:6). Suffering is also given a Christological base (1 Peter 4:13).

In Paul joy has eschatological significance (Rom. 5:2). But in Paul joy is also the actualization of freedom which takes concrete form in fellowship (Rom. 12:15). Joy is an essential factor in the relation between Paul and his churches. He asks the Roman church to pray that he might come with joy (Rom. 15:32). This joy is reciprocal (2 Cor. 2:3). It is a matter of more than mood, for it is joy "in the Lord" (Phil. 3:1; 4:4, 10). This joy looks forward to the Parousia. The future heavenly joy is being experienced already now. Since it is "joy in the faith" (Phil. 1:25), it includes readiness for martyrdom. Physical destruction will not destroy it.

In John's gospel fulfilment and joy are related to the person of Jesus. The ancient time has run its course, and the time of joy is present in Jesus (John 3:29). The close link between joy and Jesus is seen also in John 15:11. In John 16 joy and sorrow clash. The sorrow of the disciples is the joy of the world (John 15:20) because it thinks it has triumphed by destroying Jesus. Its victory, however, is only for the moment, as Jesus indicates with His metaphor of joy at the birth of a child (16:21). Christians have the promise that they have already moved from sorrow to joy. True, they experience the hatred of the world (John 15:28). Yet their joy cannot be lost, for it has the promise of being perfected (John 15:11).

Text Study of John 20:11-18

General setting of text. This has been commented on sufficiently in the Ash Wednesday sermon study.

Immediate context. The preceding verses (1-10) tell of Mary Magdalene coming to the grave while it was still dark, before the other women, of her seeing the stone rolled away and running back to tell Peter and John that the Lord's body had been taken from the tomb. Peter and John run to the tomb, Peter entering first, and verify that the tomb is indeed empty. The disciples return to their homes. Mary Magdalene comes after them to the tomb and remains outside it weeping. The following verses (19f.) contain the account of Jesus's first appearance to His disciples on the first Easter evening while they were behind locked doors. On Easter afternoon Jesus had appeared to the two disciples who were walking to Emmaus (Luke 24:13-35).

Text in vernacular. There are no significant variations in the English translations. The NAS perhaps catches the meaning of verse 17 best with "Stop clinging to Me," where most of the other translations have "Do not hold Me."

Text in original. V. 11. *Parekupsen* means peeped or peered as she was weeping (imperfect).

V. 12. Had been lying (imperfect).

V. 13. Note the personal pronoun "my" Lord, an expression of Mary's personal relationship to and love for the Lord whom she thought to be dead.

V. 14. Perhaps she turned herself back because she instinctively felt a presence behind her.

V. 15. Jesus asked her the same question the angels had asked. She was audibly sobbing in grief. Jesus adds the question, "Whom are you seeking?" He desires to focus her attention on the living rather than the dead.

V. 16. There was something about the way in which Jesus spoke her name that caused Mary to recognize Him instantly. Mary's response in turn (John retains the original Aramaic and translates with "Teacher") indicates that she had indeed seen the risen Christ.

V. 17. *Mē mou haptou* is a negative with present imperative and thus literally means "cease clinging to Me." Jesus checks Mary's impulsive eagerness and thereby reminds her that she will not now lose Him, but also that Jesus has not come back into His former life to go on with that as before. *Oupō gar* is a negative adverb of time (not yet) with perfect tense indicating Jesus is here only because He has not yet gone to His Father.

V. 18. The present tense (she comes and she announces) makes her action vivid. Her mood has changed completely from grief to joy. Yet the disciples did not believe Mary's story or the story of the other women (Mark 16:11; Luke 24:11). Mary is the first one to have seen the risen Christ.

Doctrinal study. Mary knows Christ's voice as He utters her name. The sheep know the voice of the Good Shepherd.

She will not long have Christ's physical presence. She must learn to walk by faith.

Christ was delivered for our offenses and raised again for our justification (Rom. 4:25). He is declared to be the Son of God with power according to the Spirit of holiness by His resurrection from the dead (Rom. 1:4). The resurrection is the Father's attestation of Christ's work on the cross.

Law: Without Jesus there is despair, for the hope of salvation is gone. Had Jesus remained dead, there would be reason to weep.

Gospel: Jesus knows His believers by name, individually and personally. Even though He cannot stay physically with them, He has not left them. Jesus' resurrection is news worth sharing.

Parallel passages. The only Gospel parallel is Mark 16:9-11, verses which are not found in the older more reliable manuscripts. Other parallel passages have already been given in the word study and in the doctrinal study. James 1:2 could be added.

Central thought. Jesus by His word and presence transforms Mary's grief to joy.

Homiletical Treatment

Goal-malady-means approach. The goal is that the hearers will experience more of that joy which has its source in Christ. The malady is that we often think of joy only as an emotional exuberance caused by something good. The means to the goal is Christ's resurrection which guarantees our victory over changing and sorrowful circumstances.

Sermon outline. Introduction: We all know what it feels like to be joyous because everything is going well or because a longed-for goal has been reached. The joy I want to talk to you about today is not just bubbling exuberance or emotional delight. The joy our text brings out is not merely outward cheer but inward change. That kind of joy has its source in Christ.

Mary didn't have to make herself joyful. She didn't have to pretend joy. Her joy was the natural offspring of Christ's resurrection.

And so it is with us today. The risen Christ through His Spirit now gives us joy. We celebrate today because

THE FRUIT OF THE SPIRIT IS JOY

I. The fruit of the Spirit is a joy that is based on Christ's resurrection.
  A. Christ's resurrection assures our forgiveness.
  B. Christ's resurrection gives us hope.
  C. Christ's resurrection means that He is with us always. If we want to experience more of the joy the Spirit gives, we will need to remind ourselves that Jesus lives. Joy is based on Christ's resurrection.
II. The fruit of the Spirit is a joy that is based on Christ's permanence.
  A. Christ will never change.
  B. Joy in such a Lord is permanent too.
  C. We can be joyful in all circumstances.

Conclusion: The way to maintain joy is to let the Holy Spirit by an act of Spirit-to-spirit resuscitation transfer to our own spirits Christ-centered, lasting joy. Then we can celebrate. Oh, how we can celebrate, not just today but always!

Thematic approach. The change in Mary is made the theme of a sermon that deals with the new existence of the Christian.

Sermon outline. Introduction: In her broken-hearted weeping Mary seemed unconsolable. She had lost Christ and with Him salvation. But when Christ revealed Himself, Mary was transformed. In her we see what happens to the person who has been touched by the living Christ.

WE ARE RENEWED
THROUGH THE RESURRECTION OF CHRIST

I. We have a new attitude toward God.
  A. We regard God not as an impersonal diety but as our God and our Father.
  B. We do not think of Him as far removed from our sorrows but as One who is actually present with us.
  C. We do not try to apprehend Him by our senses or our feelings, but we grasp Him by faith as our Savior and Lord.
II. We have a new attitude toward people.
  A. We see each person as important (Christ singles people out by name).
  B. We perceive that it is our duty to say to people the Gospel that Jesus has said to us.
  C. We are willing to perform this duty (Mary went) among relatives and friends, through the local congregation.

Conclusion: The resurrection of Christ makes a difference in our lives. There is a transformation from sorrow to joy that is reflected in a new attitude toward God and people.

Life-experience-oriented approach. The sermon is shaped by the text's encounter with the grief experience of the preacher and of the hearers.

Sermon outline. Introduction: It is natural to weep at the time of death. I have, and no doubt you have too. It's painful to think that a familiar form will never again appear in the doorway and a dear voice will never again be heard in the room.

Christ's death brought pain to Mary. She expressed her pain and grief by weeping. But Mary experienced something that dried her tears. She found consolation in a living Lord. So do we.

HE LIVES TO WIPE AWAY MY TEARS

I. Jesus lives to remind us that God is our Father.
   A. Jesus' resurrection proves that our sins can no longer separate us from God.
   B. While God is Jesus' Father by nature, God is our Father by Jesus' mediation. As our Father, God loves us steadily, even when death causes us grief.
II. Jesus lives to assure us of His presence.
   A. Because Jesus is alive, He is able to be with all Christians everywhere.
   B. In times of grief we may not recognize Him; yet His presence makes it possible for the sorrow to work for our good in the days ahead.
III. Jesus lives to bring us to Himself in heaven.
   A. As Jesus lived and died for us, so He rose from the grave and ascended to heaven for us.
   B. His resurrection guarantees our resurrection from the grave, and His ascension confirms our rising to be with His God and our God forever.

Conclusion: Death brings tears to us as it did to Mary. But we never have to sorrow as those who have no hope. There is consolation because Jesus lives to wipe away my tears.

Sermon Illustrations

Some of the wait-until-you-get-to-heaven-to-enjoy-life crowd feel that all of life must be solemn and serious. Others feel it's okay to be happy—*unless* you are doing something religious. There's the mother who said to her child: "Stop smiling so much! You're in church," (Eldon Weisheit, "The Fruit of the Spirit is Joy," *The Lutheran Witness,* October 28, 1973, p. 5.)

How awful to be told that you have to be joyful! Being miserable is bad enough without having to feel guilty about it. Pretending joy is a burden. What a strain to sing Hallelujah while thinking, "I sure feel lousy!" How artificial to see a smile pasted on a grim life. (Weisheit, "Joy," p. 5)

Beneath the perpetual smile of modern man lurks the grimace of despair. (Reinhold Niebuhr)

We are rather like characters in a book. God is the author, Christ the hero, and we are his followers. We have been given, by the grace of God, a peek of the last page of the last chapter and we see that in the end Christ triumphs, the devil is defeated, and all pain and sorrow and tears done away with forever. And, wonder of wonders, we are there in the last chapter, sharing the joy of the victory with Christ. Meantime, however, we are back here in our own chapter, somewhere in the middle of the book—and we don't know what it holds for us. We don't even know how many chapters there are between ours and the end of the book. We simply know that in ours there are battles going on, wounds being sustained, risks that must be taken—we're right in the thick of it. But we're not alone—Christ, the hero, the one who will win in the end, is by our side. Our joy and our confidence is sure because we've seen the last chapter. (Guder, p. 43)

We may dig so deeply for wounds that we think need healing that we end up making them worse. I believe we help each other more simply by enjoying and appreciating each other. (Guder, p. 45)

It is rather insulting to God to keep on bringing up old troubles, as if he couldn't deal with them and as if the good things he constantly gives us were hardly worth noticing compared to the hard knocks we've had.

The really remarkable thing about this world is how much joy God has managed to put into it in spite of its sin and stupidity. He not only redeemed it and offers us all the joys of heaven, but he has provided for our pleasure— yes, pleasure—unnumbered joys right now. (Guder, p. 46)

When, because of care or sorrow, Luther found himself downcast and cheerless, he would dispel his despondency by crying out to himself, "Vivit!" Latin for "He lives!" Many times he seized a piece of chalk and wrote this Vivit on his study table, and more than once friends entered his room to find the wall and doors covered with Vivit. And when someone asked him why he did this, he answered: "Jesus lives, and if He were not among the living, I would not wish to live even an hour; but because He lives, we shall live through him, as he himself says, 'Because I live, you shall live also,'" (Oswald Riess, *Everlasting Arms,* [Ernest Kaufmann, Inc., 1949], p. 86)

Part II:
Sermons
by Kenneth Rogahn

Gentleness from the Passion of Christ

John 13:3-5 (1-17)

Introduction

Certain words in the English language sound like what they mean. Such is the word *gentle* or *gentleness*. The sound of the word is soft to our ears, and it even sounds gentle, to emphasize the meaning. We talk about someone or something being gentle as a lamb, which brings to mind images of softness and fluffiness. A man who is pleasant to be with, not harsh or gruff, would be considered a "gentleman."

Jesus was a "gentle" man. He shows us that gentle does not mean soft in the sense of weak or bland. When Jesus or Christians are described with the word relating to gentleness, it is a compliment and tribute to their kindness and a recognition of their quiet and self-assured strength. We see a gentle Jesus in the text for today, which tells how Jesus washed the disciples' feet. This text is often associated with Maundy Thursday, the night when Jesus was betrayed and the time when He gave His disciples the command to "love one another as I have loved you." But it is appropriate also on Ash Wednesday, at the start of the Lenten season, that we recognize how Jesus was gentle in life and in death. As again this year we recall the well-known events and statements in the Passion Story, we may feel only like spectators and listeners. The experiences of Jesus in His suffering, death, and resurrection may not seem directly related to our daily life as Christians today. But God's Spirit, who called us to faith in Christ, will also sanctify us by His Word. The power of God's Spirit at work in us produces the fruit of faith in our lives. So today and in the coming weeks of Lent we will be linking "the fruit of the Spirit," which Paul lists in Galatians 5:22, with the various episodes in Jesus' Passion. Today we combine the account of Jesus washing the disciples' feet with the fruit of *Gentleness*. Jesus loved His disciples throughout His lifelong association with them. And He "loved His own to the end," verse 1 of the Scripture reading says. Gentleness, for Jesus and His followers, is a life and death attitude.

I. Jesus Was a Gentle Man

Jesus' kindness toward His disciples, which He demonstrated in His act of foot washing and the explanation of its significance, was a kindness that proceeded from a position of power. We read in verse 3 of the text that Jesus "knew" that everything was under His control. He knew that He had come from God and would return to God. His attitude was not snobbery, but a sense of self-awareness that moved Him to action. He decided He would not remain *above* them, but He put Himself at their feet.

A. His Deeds Were Humble

Jesus washed the feet of all the disciples with tender, loving care. Despite the awkwardness of the moment and their apparent embarrassment, He was determined to make them clean. With a gentle cleansing and wiping He removed the dirt and soil of the day. Jesus is the supreme example of one who "stoops to conquer." Instead of considering others as beneath Him or refusing to lower Himself to the gentle service of helping, He puts Himself at their feet and makes them clean. He is, of course, above and beyond all men, this One who came from the Father, but nobody would have guessed it from the way He acted or from what He said. With water and towel, like a servant, He washed their feet.

B. His Words Were Gentle Too

And then Peter objected—Peter, the spokesman for the Twelve and so often also for us. He didn't know what this foot washing was all about, but that didn't stop Peter from objecting. Peter was so much the opposite of the gentle Jesus. Peter was the assertive and aggressive leader. He knew about power and power plays. We can almost hear him boasting, "Nobody out-humbles me!" And he told Jesus that He could not wash his feet.

Jesus' reply was firm, but still gentle. With "friendly persuasion" He explained why His actions were necessary. His cleansing of them was a sign of the bond between Him and them, an imparting of His holiness to them. He would take away their sin and personal uncleanness. The washing symbolized that cleansing and also gave them an example for their future relationships. With calm insistence He continued washing as He spoke. Paul states in 2 Timothy that such correction (with gentleness) is the kind of instruction that leads to repentance. Easy gentleness is so much better for both parties than the harsh confrontation and chewing out which we may equate with correction. Jesus shows that it is indeed a "soft answer," a gentle reply, that averts wrath and anger. We find it easier to rebuke sharply or sarcastically when others challenge us in our efforts to help. Jesus taught Peter that gentleness does not result from putting others down and pulling rank on them. People are not better off by our insistence on controlling them. Jesus' approach is otherwise, although the world may consider it foolishness.

II. So I Can Be a "Gentleman's Gentleman"

Jesus knew His real status, as the disciples also recognized: they called Him "Lord" and "Teacher" in verse 13 of the Scripture reading. And so He was! But the title that He prized was not the glorious label but the simple one of

"Servant." In the terminology of the genteel, He chose to be a "gentleman's gentleman."

A. Jesus Served All Others

Servants must be gentle with those they serve. Gentleness is an attribute of people who want to be helpful and truly good in the lives of others. Jesus was a king, as He had been acclaimed when He rode into Jerusalem on Palm Sunday. But even on the day of glory there were already intimations that it should be called Passion Sunday, for He came as one who was humble and gentle as the prophet Zechariah had anticipated and as the apostle Matthew later explained. Jesus accepted the dirty job of cleansing sins, and more than easy words are required to remove the deeply ingrained stains. More was needed than a mild aromatic scent to cleanse hands that did evil and feet that walked into sin. We see that His greatness consisted in the fact that Jesus did not "put down" other people—even when they were in error. So also His greatness was shown when He "put up" Himself, on the cross, to bear people's sins. Like a lamb led to the slaughter (as "gentle as a lamb," we said), He moved on quietly until He came to the cross of cleansing and took away the sins of the world. As Jesus waited on people the night before for their benefit, so He waited on the Lord on Good Friday. Jesus served the Father and trusted God to deliver Him. In the same way that the directions on the label of a car wash detergent may recommend working in the shade, so the dead body of Jesus was laid in a grave and passed through the valley of the shadow of death. In that tomb's coolness the atonement that was accomplished on the cross could turn into the glorious "shine" of a glorified body.

B. We Serve Others Too

And then He rose from the grave. He is alive now. He is present with us. He who has almighty power comes to us. The apostle Paul learned to deal with his people "by the meekness and gentleness of Christ," who displayed a face-to-face humility and gentleness that helps others. Paul gave the readers of 1 Corinthians a choice: he would come to them with a rod of discipline or in gentleness (whatever they preferred). Jesus is that gentle Man who comes to help us be like Him. He has a gentle touch. In times when we minister to the physical, emotional, and spiritual needs of others, Jesus' Spirit strengthens us to do so gently and for their well-being. When we correct error, the Spirit of Christ helps us. Listen to the tone as well as the content of speech. How gentle can we be?

Jesus had said, "Blessed are the meek, the gentle" in the Beatitudes. In His resurrection He gives power over all the earth to those who are gentle like Him. This is a fulfilment of the psalm that says, "The meek shall possess the land." He makes us wise as He is wise so that we not only talk about how others are to be treated but we show it and do it with gentleness. The wise man, James says, is the gentle man. Paul says in Galatians that a Christian restores with gentleness the brother who has drifted into sin. Gentle Christians know what they believe and gladly confess their faith, but they do even that with gentleness and reverence. So give witness to Jesus Christ in the loving and winning manner that His Spirit directs.

Now we understand why Christ washed the disciples' feet. We have also come to understand how we are to live. We can live and serve as He did, and we can share in His life-style and power. He is speaking to His church and to His people today when He says, "Come unto Me." We imitate Him because His yoke *is* easy and He *is* gentle with us. Listen to that Word and receive it with meekness. It will produce new life and new activity, life and actions like His. Women, as well as men, can be imitators of the gentle Jesus and display the true beauty of a "gentle and quiet spirit." For gentleness is the mark of God's people. Paul exhorts his readers in Colossians: "Put on then, as God's chosen ones, holy and beloved, compassion, kindness, lowliness, *meekness,* and patience, forbearing one another." Such is the fruit of faith, the style of people who have been cleansed by Jesus.

Conclusion

To be gentle in an aristocratic and genealogical sense of the word is to be wellborn, to be refined and not coarse. Such a gentle manner is seen in those of noble birth who are the men and women who have been "born again" by water and Spirit. Such a person, Luther says, is not easily provoked to anger, either by the needs or the objections of others.

We "Gentiles" need special urging these New Testament days to demonstrate the gentleness of Christ, which is the fruit of the Spirit. In Jesus' days on earth, Jews regularly provided for the washing of feet of those who came as visitors to their houses. It was a social amenity and custom that was not easily neglected. Our gentle service to others has no such cultural support, especially with those who most need cleansing today. But we have made a "gentleman's agreement" with our Lord. And so we are bound, not by law or regulation, but by honor and desire. We lower ourselves to help others, as He has already done for them and for us. We say good-bye and good riddance to the world's notion that raw power is greatness and that the one who is served ranks highest. Our Lord teaches and tells and shows and proves: to be great—like Him—is to be gentle. We are to serve and even to correct—as He did—with gentleness. We act and do it in His Spirit. Gentleness is His first gift to us this holy season.

Lent 2

Patience from the Passion of Christ

Matt. 26:36-46

Introduction

Picture a hospital waiting room. The patient has been taken elsewhere, and so the family sits and waits. Or the new patient sits in the admitting office, waiting for the endless paperwork to be completed before being taken to his room. Or the patient lies in bed, expecting the doctor to come in with a report on recent tests. Change the scene to a restaurant. A woman has ordered her meal and after a lengthy wait begins to wonder when or if the waiter is going to bring it. Or your car is in the garage. The repairman has promised to call you when the work is done or if there are major repairs needed. So you listen all day for the phone to ring. All these examples remind us of the delays in our lives. We wait! And we wait some more. And then we wait even longer. Attempts at being patient soon lead to paralysis, and we can't seem to do anything else while we're waiting.

Perhaps we pray that well-known prayer, "Lord, give me patience, and give it to me *right now.*" We have to learn that it takes time to develop patience and there are things for us to do while we are waiting on others. Waiting may be monotonous, even irritating, as hour after hour of our lives sounds more and more like the repeated verses of the song, "A hundred bottles of beer on the wall...." But we need to have patience. How do we get it?

I. We Can Be Patient with Others

Patience begins with the certainty that there is a plan, and timing, behind what is happening. The song about the bottles of beer maybe boring, but at least we know that eventually we come to "two bottles of beer on the wall," then finally to "one bottle," and THEN it will be over, and we will have reached the end.

A. All Proceeds According to God's Will

In the same way, believers accept *in principle* that God is in charge of everything that happens. The scene of Jesus praying in the Garden of Gethsemane presents this truth when He prays, "Thy will be done." God is by definition Master and Controller of everything that happens and all that will yet happen. Events proceed according to His great and loving plan. God is not dead. He is still in charge. So we also believe and say. We have a trust and reliance that the events of life are an unfolding of God's plans. Each time we say the Lord's Prayer we confess this confidence with the petition, "Thy will be done on earth as it is in heaven."

The prophets certainly believed that God was in control, and they spoke that message to others. But not everything came to pass at once for them either, so they had to verify their preaching by "suffering and patience" as James says. In Acts we read how Paul was ready on one occasion to lay out God's plan for the benefit of King Agrippa. In so doing he had to ask the king to listen *patiently*. Events do not all come together immediately. It is not unusual for God's people to experience delay, which may seem to contradict their expectation.

B. But We Become Impatient

And so we become impatient, especially with other people, when things don't seem to proceed at all according to our preconceived plan. Paul, for example, has to urge the leaders in Thessalonica to be patient with the idle and fainthearted and weak. James tells us to be like the farmer, who waits patiently for rain and harvest. Many others before us, all the Old Testament believers, had to wait patiently to receive the fulfilment of what was promised. But it is so hard to be patient. The example of others is inadequate.

The three disciples who accompanied Jesus to His place of prayer knew that God was Lord of all. But they individually fell prey to fatigue and frustration as they waited for Jesus. They fell asleep. We too fail and fall asleep in one way or another. We quit waiting on the Lord because, finally, we become impatient with His timetable and with His way of doing things—or, as we would complain, His way of NOT doing things. So we are tempted to do things our way.

Although we rejoice in forgiveness and say that we are to forgive others, in truth we can't wait for the opportunity to get even with those who fail us. We aren't patient with failures. Like the unforgiving servant of Jesus' parable who wouldn't forgive though he had been forgiven, we won't wait for others to make up for their mistakes. If the law is on our side, we demand resolution of the difficulty *at once*. But (Paul said) love is patient and kind, and patience is a mark of God's people. In Ephesians Paul encourages Christians "to lead a life worthy of the calling to which you have been called, with all lowliness and meekness, with *patience,* forbearing one another in love." The children of God, as Martin Luther describes them, wait patiently for some improvement in those who have harmed them (*Lectures on Galatians,* ed. Jaroslav Pelikan, *Luther's Works,* American Edition, vol. 27 [St. Louis: CPH, 1964], p. 94). Yes, we know we should. Of course, we wish we could. We'd like to obey, just as the disciples wanted to be supportive of Jesus. But their problem is also our problem: "The Spirit is willing, but the flesh is weak." How can we expect to be patient *now*? Our very situation makes us more impatient.

II. God Is Patient with Us

It is a lonely business, to wait on the Lord. It is hard to keep busy and to make sense of things during the hours of waiting. The card game, solitaire, or patience, may help us pass the time, but does passing the time change anything? Or does it get us anywhere just to while away the time? What else can we do?

A. Jesus Prayed and Did God's Will

We can pray as Jesus did. But that too may take a degree of patience that we often do not possess or might call for a concentration that we don't have anymore. Fortunately, our prayer is included in Jesus' prayer, when He said to the Father, "Nevertheless, Thy will be done." God's will was done then, on earth as it is in heaven, because when Jesus had finished speaking, He waited patiently for the enemy to arrive and to arrest Him. He was patient when they put Him on trial, while He was crucified, patient until He was dead. Jesus patiently waited for "the axe to fall," for judgment to come, for the final reckoning of accounts to be made. And then it was time for Him to pay all, to "pay what *thou* owest." God's patience finally reached its limit. God's will called for sin to be dealt with. God's anger came to the boiling point. His wrath was displayed. His patience ran out.

And Jesus was there on the cross to bear it. He was patient with each step of God's plan. He knew and trusted the Word of His Father, and He carried it out. When He was hanged out there on Calvary, He was still patient enough to "hang in there" and satisfy the Father's good pleasure by doing His will. Into death and even beyond, from the hour that finally was at hand until the new day that dawned on Easter when He rose again, Jesus was patient and obedient.

B. God Still Works on Us and Others

Now the Father is patient with sinners whom His Son has redeemed, and that includes everyone. We read in 2 Peter that God's apparent delay in acting can give people time to repent and can lead to their eventual salvation. It is God's gracious nature to be patient and "slow to anger," even as He was with backsliding Israel. He is patient even as He was with downsliding disciples, as in the garden called Gethsemane and the other garden where they found the empty tomb on Easter. He is patient even with us and does not strike out to destroy us, for His hand of judgment fell heavily on our Savior at the cross.

We are encouraged by the Spirit of God not to quit on other people, not to give up hope of what God has in store for them. As the contemporary motto has it, "Be patient; God's not done with me yet." What Jesus said has always been true, and still is true today, "My Father is always working, and I am working!" So we also can do the Father's will while we await final deliverance. Look at the example of Paul. Who of us would have worked with Paul as patiently as God did until Paul was finally called to faith? Paul knew that he was meant to be an example to others, as he declares: "Knowing how patiently God has dealt with me makes me able to be patient with others." In time, God makes that happen in all of His people. Give Him time to work in you, and give others time to experience His grace through you.

77

Conclusion

To know God's patience means to follow and imitate that patience. The Spirit of Christ makes it happen. So much of our life is spent in a seemingly helpless situation of waiting, where "all we can do is pray" and hope for God's will to be done. But we can wait with the same kind of confidence and expectation as those who wait in the obstetrical ward of a hospital. There must be labor and prospective parents must have patience until the time comes. But when the new life arrives we see that it was worth waiting for. Look again at the key word in our meditation. In one spelling, P-A-T-I-E-N-C-E, it is that powerful fruit of the Spirit that God causes to grow in us. But one can also spell the word, P-A-T-I-E-N-T-S, and that reminds us that we are patients in need of healing. Our frustration and doubt are symptoms of a lack of trust that God will carry out His saving will. And patients like us need a remedy for our impatience. With only a minimum of imagination, we can separate the abbreviation for a prescription (RX) and rearrange the letters into the XP symbol (the Chi-Rho). We remember that we who are sick to death with human impatience are helped by the heavenly Physician who can make us well. He promises to give us complete care, and we will trust and wait until God's good and gracious will is done. Jesus will do it in us. He will save others through us. And He has as much patience as is needed for all this to happen. So will we, by the gift of this fruit of the Spirit.

Lent 3

Faithfulness from the Passion of Christ

Matt. 26:47-56

Introduction

The term *faith* is dear to the hearts of all Christians. We know that we are saved "by faith alone." But do we realize that this word, faith, as used in the Scriptures, is many faceted? To define faith as an intellectual agreement with the teachings of the Bible is not an adequate definition. There is much more to faith than that. One aspect of the term that is at times omitted by us is better expressed by translating the word as "faith*fulness.*" In modern electronic language, we talk about fidelity, even high fidelity. A high-fidelity reproduction of sound is what we expect on present-day recording systems, i.e., the sound produced is expected to be an accurate presentation of the original. Such high-fidelity means being true to the original. This idea can give us an understanding of faithfulness as a fruit of God's Spirit. Faithfulness means reliability and dependability in dealing with other people. It is a gift from God that makes us like God in that others can count on us to do and to be what we say. We keep our promises. We are not talking about faith *in* God, but a faithfulness *to* God that is directed toward our fellow human beings. Martin Luther focuses on the word in the text in the same way, as faithfulness to people, not to God. The question is: How do we treat others? What is our attitude toward one another? Or simply, are we faithful?

I. We Are Unfaithful Under Stress

Loyalty to others and acceptance of obligations are marks of a person who responds to God's call for love to the neighbor. He commands us to be faithful.

A. We Don't Believe the Word Is Effective

We find it difficult if not impossible to obey what God has said. We are impulsive and reckless in our attempts to make things happen the way we think they ought to be, regardless of what God has said. Recall the events in the Garden of Gethsemane when the crowd came to arrest Jesus. Judas had been with Jesus in His earthly ministry and had heard more than once the necessity for God's people, and God's Son, to carry out the will of God. But, for some unexplained reason, he took the matter into his own hands and was determined to make things happen in a certain way. Perhaps he was a disgruntled loyalist, perhaps an eager advocate, perhaps something else, but Judas was not being faithful to his Master and was not true to his promise to follow Him. The kiss he planted on Jesus' cheek was a token of infidelity, not a warm welcome and acknowledgment of affection and admiration. His empty action contradicted any pledge of allegiance to his Lord. The other disciple (another evangelist tells us it was Peter) was no better, for he struck out with a sword and wounded a servant. What madness! What foolishness! What infidelity! Such behavior did no good for the other person. Jesus had met Judas' treachery with a calm greeting, calling him, "friend." But Peter had to get things under control. He got things going in the only way things get done in this world, by reckless action. Jesus rebuked him: violence is not the answer. The sword is no solution, only a catalyst, to danger. God said, "Love your neighbor," but humankind refuses to abide by the word of the faithful God and instead sets its own course.

B. We Don't Live by the Word but Abandon It

The other disciples failed in another way. They proved unfaithful not by action but by inaction. Did they stand by their Lord and Teacher? Would they suffer with Him? Did they align themselves boldly by His side for all to see? They did not. They fled! We too find it easier to abandon those in need than to stand with them. Jesus remembered the Father's promise, and they had heard it too. "Legions of angels" would protect the child of God the text says in verse 53. The disciples seemed to respond, "Come on, angels. You do it, then. As for us, we're leaving. Let the angels protect Jesus." What an abuse of the Lord's Word. What a denial of the promise. What an emptying of the power that protects us. The disciples gave up on the possibility of any solution and broke faith with God's Word. In such dangerous circumstances we can objectively appreciate their cool-headed and cold-hearted calculations. But this is unbelief. This is despair. This is infidelity. And so nobody stands firm and relies on God's promise to come true.

II. God Is Faithful in Christ

No one was faithful but Jesus. Jesus remained in the garden, alone and faithful. He stayed, not because He couldn't overcome the enemy, nor because he wasn't tempted to lash out or to flee. Jesus remained within their grasp because He was *faithful*. He was determined to prove that what God has said was true. He did that instead of turning aside or changing God's plan.

A. Jesus Was Faithful for Us

"It must be so," Jesus said in verse 54. The divine necessity of His arrest, His eventual condemnation, and His death was not to be avoided. "Jesus lived and died in order to fulfil the Scriptures of the prophets," the text explains. It was His mission to live out in faithful and inerrant reproduction every direction in the plan which brought humankind back to God. Matthew testifies faithfully that Jesus both acted and suffered in obedience to the written outline of the Father's will. "It is written!" God promised. It must be so. There can be no doubt, for the One who spoke is faithful.

Daily and openly Jesus had exhibited an honest obedience to the Father with God's Word as His guide and power. He was no secret Savior, no hidden Hope, no unseen Ultimatum. He resolved to show and to go God's way, even to death on the cross. He could depend on the Lord with confidence, even when those around Him repeated like a broken record, "Crucify Him! Crucify Him!" He was true to the Father and kept His Father's Word in His heart even when the chorus of taunters drowned out His prayers and choked out the breath from His body. His perfect love was focused on that hope that was yet to be realized by people of faith. 1 Cor. 13:13 indicates that "faith, hope, love abide, these three; but the greatest of these is love." Jesus lived out these words. He was true to the end.

B. Jesus Is Faithful in Us

Now we can take God seriously. We see that He really means what He said. His Word is true, regardless of all the lies that object. Jesus' death on the cross underwrites and guarantees the Father's welcome to all. His suffering and death for me is the foundation on which my hope is built. Jesus Christ is risen from the dead, as the Father had promised—it must be so! We are plugged into that recording of God's salvation history that is played out in the cross and resurrection of Jesus. As we take up our cross daily and follow Him, God is faithful daily with His word of forgiveness to us. He is faithful because He gives us Jesus who in every temptation is "the Way of escape" from the power of evil. Our faithful God inspires us to be faithful unto death and to receive the crown of life. Paul writes to Timothy that even he in his youth could be an example of faithfulness by his speech and in conduct, by what he said and what he did. No one is too young or too old. Faithfulness is the fruit of the Spirit, and through Jesus Christ we are made trustworthy people. When we promise to do good for others, our neighbor can rely on us to come through with help. We will be true to our word and to God's Word.

Conclusion

The exalted Christ speaks to His church in the book of Revelation, "I know your works, your faith, your patient endurance." The Lord gives us demands but also promises. The Christian life begins with a faith that receives and lives by the word of promise in Jesus. The life of Jesus is reproduced faithfully and manifested in a chain of other qualities in our lives. It keeps us from being ineffective or unfruitful in the knowledge of our Lord Jesus Christ. We read in 2 Peter that we are to "make every effort to supplement [our] *faith* with virtue...and knowledge...and self-control...and steadfastness...and godliness ...and brotherly affection with love." The basis of the sequence is faithfulness, being rocklike and stable in reliance on God's Word to us.

In simple terms, faith works in a double sense. Faith in Christ makes us children of God, renewed in His image. But true faith is not so internal that it is hidden from sight and not an influence on others. Faithfulness is personal belief connected to daily reality and brought to expression by visible acts of love. Faith and love go together. Faith is and love does. Paul commended his friend Philemon and his co-worker Timothy three times for their love as demonstrations of faith. In the motto of the United States Marine Corps, to be a believer is to be *"semper fidelis":* always faithful. We are always faithful to the Lord and always faithfully carrying out His commands. In deeds of care and helpfulness for people, the fruit of faithfulness can be seen by all and will be praised by God as well.

Lent 4

Goodness from the Passion of Christ

Matt. 26:57-68

Introduction

In the old-time Western movies, the good guys always wore white hats while the bad guys wore black hats. As we grew out of childhood, we learned that life's values are not always that easy to identify. In fact, white hats and black hats don't tell us much about people or circumstances that we encounter in life. There is another more subtle truth to be noted here as well. A simple dividing line between good and bad does not take account of the various degrees of goodness or badness in the world. There is a great deal of room for either more or less of either quality. Something is often better or worse in relation to something else, rather than being absolutely the best or the worst. We see shades of gray between black and white extremes. Furthermore it is often easier to distinguish good and bad in theory than in practice. We may talk about what is good or bad in the abstract, but in everyday circumstances neither good nor bad is so easily identifiable.

I. Our Attempts at Goodness Turn to Badness

We all have some definite ideas about right and wrong, or good and bad, of course. But they are often very subjective and individualized. We assume that what *we* think is good must really be good. And yet we've been wrong too many times to trust our personal judgment completely. We too easily end up in situations that are bad or can even be mad, although we had started out thinking that they were good.

A. Human Ideas of Goodness Result in Bad Actions

Sometimes the confusion or error develops because we have the right form but the action is not true goodness. We can justify or explain ourselves and what we're doing by saying, "It's good for you." Notice, for example, some of the characters in today's portion of the Passion Story who were mistreating Jesus. The evildoers could defend their actions as attempts at pursuing goodness. The tormentors could present good motives for their behavior. But they were caught and revealed in the evil and madness of the moment.

Caiaphas could say that he was only trying to preserve the religion of his people. The questions he asked of Jesus at His trial were intended to bring out the truth. As a religious leader it was his duty to protect the flock from error. His questions to Jesus led him to the conclusion that Jesus deserved to die, and he probably condemned Jesus with a clear conscience and a feeling of personal goodness. The witnesses who spoke against Jesus likewise could explain that they only sought to eliminate a criminal from society, to remove Him from the everyday scene. They may have had to stretch the truth a bit and perhaps twisted the words Jesus had originally spoken, but what was the difference as long as "justice" prevailed and goodness as they perceived it was upheld? Those others who abused Jesus, with spitting and striking and slapping to punctuate their taunts, might have believed that they were pursuing a God-pleasing work by teaching Jesus a lesson and by providing a warning to others like Him who had no respect for law and religion. He seemed to be a rebel, and certainly He was in error. How could there be anything wrong in mistreating Him? They found no goodness in Him that would move them to apologize for their mistreatment.

B. We Also See Only Badness in People

Listen to the judgment the priest pronounces on Jesus. Who wouldn't find it easy to agree with his verdict, given all the circumstances? To talk the way Jesus did is blasphemy! For one to identify oneself with God and with one of His divine agents, when one is a mere mortal (with no particular record of religious goodness, at that) is clearly to put one's life in jeopardy. In such a case as this, death is deserved. The decision of the council is substantiated in Leviticus, from "the *good* book," where the Lord commanded, "He who blasphemes the name of the Lord shall be put to death." Once the first stone has been thrown, it is easy for the rest of us to pitch in. If the "guardians of goodness," the religious leaders, can condemn someone, doesn't it just prove how bad humankind in general is and how correct it is to deal harshly with the bad elements of society? When someone is "down and out" and under attack by other righteous citizens, all of whom are good people, the intolerant rejection of what is bad makes sense.

Old Testament believers were well aware of God's demand for goodness. The prophet Micah summarized it so well when he concluded that what God requires is for man to "do good." With a standard like that before our eyes, it is no great task to find the contrary-minded and to isolate violators of the ideal. On the other hand, we who listen to our conscience or any of us willing to examine the matter openly and honestly cannot deny the depth and power of evil in our personal lives. Even when others do not know, or they equate our outer goodness with an inner perfection, we know ourselves too well to agree with their opinion. "If they really knew," we think. "If they realized what I am truly like, what I actually think, they would share my self-condemnation."

But such inner judgments must be concealed and subsumed under a show of goodness. The point is that we see our own sin so clearly that we must believe that "they, too" are as bad as we are. The awareness we have of our own sin makes us suspicious and judgmental toward others. We impute evil motives to their actions and assume the worst in others. We know how quickly and how

84

easily we would take advantage of other people, and we fear that they may do the same to us. We have learned to "do unto others before they do unto us," in self-defense. We measure and evaluate others by our own self-evaluations, and that means everyone we see is bad.

II. Christ's Assumed Badness Produces Goodness in Us

But can human beings really be as bad as we think they are if God is willing to become one of us? Perhaps we are in error not only in our personal character but also in our basic perception of humanity. Doesn't the incarnation of God in Jesus Christ at least suggest that there may be some value and goodness in being a person like us? Especially if it means that someone like us, like me, can straighten out the confusion of goodness and badness that plagues us all?

A. Jesus Became Sin and Badness for Us

In our place and on our behalf, Jesus takes the badness of humankind upon Himself. He identifies so totally with our badness that, according to 2 Corinthians, He who knew no sin became sin for us. Human values and judgments suddenly cease as Jesus established a new order: "From now on...," Jesus begins in verse 64, He will be the One to decide what is good and what is bad. "Only One is good," He said during His ministry, in tribute to God in heaven. There is the test of goodness: is it of God? This good God in Jesus Christ silently accepts the death and the curse which upset all human values. Jesus on the tree of the cross bore and even became a curse, in fulfilment of God's judgment in Deuteronomy: "Cursed be every one who hangs on a tree." "God is good," even children know, and worshipers rejoice in His goodness in the words of the liturgy from 1 Chronicles, "O give thanks to the Lord, for He is good." The Psalms agree. But now God's good Word and law are turned upon Himself, and they lead to a bad death for the good Son of God who "went around doing good."

In the mystery of the cross of Christ we find gladness and comfort. And that is good for us. It was not good for Him that He had to suffer and die, but so good is His goodness that He did it for us. We are forgiven because He died bearing our sin. He removed evil from us and made us good, as God's original creation was good. When Jesus rose from the dead as the triumphant and vindicated Lord, it meant that goodness had been raised up—even though once raised up on a cross—and it showed that badness had been put down—also through the cross. We cheer, "Good for You, Jesus," as we recognize His almighty power and grace in triumph. But He corrects us, and we realize we were mixed up again! "No," He says, "My cross and resurrection are good for *you!*"

B. His Spirit Produces Real Goodness in Us

Like a seed, Jesus was buried in the ground in order that a plant might grow and could produce much fruit. This good tree of the cross, and the perfect Savior who claimed it, produces the good fruit of life like His. Our evil and sin weighed Him down with cross and tomb. By the goodness of God Jesus rose

85

again, leaving all sin behind. As we were buried with Him and raised again in our baptism, we are made like Jesus. Therefore we are made to be God's children, to grow up to be like Him. Surely "the fruit of light is found in all that is good and right and true," as Ephesians says, and that is the case with the family of God. We still have the promise of the Good Shepherd in the words of Psalm 23, now a personal reality instead of an abstract word, "Surely *goodness* and mercy shall follow me...." As Jesus shares His goodness with us because He is merciful, we are able to follow Him to new areas of helpfulness.

My being a "little Christ," as Luther called Christians, is also good for you. Israel's King Jehoiada was once acclaimed as good because he returned his people to true religion and turned them from false worship. Jesus is better because He makes this change happen in us and then in others through us. No wonder Paul was satisfied with the Roman believers who were "full of goodness" along with their knowledge. When one knows God as a gracious and loving Father, it is easier to be good to the rest of His children. God's Spirit is in us now, as we believe in Jesus Christ. His sanctifying power increased our goodness day by day, as we are nourished by Word and Sacrament. The new life which God began in us at Baptism will grow stronger under the influence of His Good Spirit, and we will produce good fruit.

Conclusion

Even a secular philosopher can recognize that

> There is so much good in the worst of us,
> And so much bad in the best of us,
> That it hardly behooves any of us
> To talk about the rest of us.

All humans are a mixture of goodness and badness, right and wrong, righteousness and evil. We Christians are, Luther reminds us, simultaneously saint and sinner. But we who may casually exclaim, "My goodness," when others say carelessly, "My God," know that it is God's goodness that is *so* good that His almighty and gracious Spirit can make us good enough to do much good. Christians are both God-receivers and God-sharers, and that is all by the goodness of God.

Lent 5

Self-control from the Passion of Christ

Matt. 26:69-75

Introduction

Imagine this scene of confusion: People rushing to and fro. Crowds in the courtyard. Words being exchanged. Shouts and cries. Questions asked. Animal sounds. Curses. Crying. Tears. Noise. Chaos! A voice asks, "Who's in charge here?" There is hesitancy and doubt when the request is made, "Take me to your leader." Is there anyone in control?

The description of the scene at Jesus' trial shows that it is a smaller copy of life itself. The confusion in the courtyard around Peter is familiar to anyone who reflects upon what the writer of Ecclesiastes calls "vanity" in life. As the bewildered Hamlet confesses, "The times are out of joint." So little in life seems purposeful or under control. Whether it's cars or kids, a situation with no control or that is out-of-control leads to disaster. But just as certainly, too tight control can lead to a crack-up. Just enough direction, not too much correction, is needed. What a challenge. No wonder there is confusion, even silence, when someone asks the question, "Who is in control?"

I. The World Has Gone out of Control

Life is like a runaway animal or machine. Once started, once released from restraint, the rush is pell-mell and panicky. With no sense of goals, almost no awareness of consequences, the world and its inhabitants move along. In the old days school report cards used to grade students on self-control along with other virtues. What grade would we give ourselves today?

A. Cosmic Influences Threaten Us

How would Peter have evaluated himself that night in the courtyard—before he was confronted by the people around him? Like most of us, he felt capable, self-assured. He could handle things, he thought. He'd be all right. And then the trouble began. First questions, then accusations. Bit by bit his self-control was attacked and crumbled. "Weren't you...? Aren't you...? Didn't you...?" The questioners around him were so positive in their inquisitions. One word wouldn't satisfy them. More words were too many. Peter couldn't speak up, but he couldn't be silent either. He moved away, sought a calmer place. But there was no escape.

There's no place in this world where a person is safe from attacks like that. Call it fate, the devil, the powers that be, evil, spiritual forces. Something seems to conspire to push us into a corner and seal every avenue of escape. One minute everything is reasonably sure. The next, doubt and anxiety take over. Something chips away at our ego, our character, our personality. People and forces that we can't control close in on us. We become tongue-tied like Peter, finally free only to stammer and lie and twist or avoid the truth in a vain attempt to put things in order.

B. Personal Weaknesses Direct Us

The blustering and posturing we resort to further expose the emptiness within. We curse ourselves and the day we were born. We condemn the circumstances that brought us to this point, perhaps we even critize the God who (we think) should have prevented this examination from happening to us. We swear that what is said is true or assert that the charges are not true. We swear that the lie is true. We swear we're not lying when we distort the truth. Even the best do it, so why should we consider ourselves immune? King David was guilty of lying with Bathsheba and then lying for her. Finally he even was lying about her to himself until the prophet brings him to reality with the abrupt accusation, "You are the man!" Then David had no place to go, no words to excuse or defend himself. His sin had let his life get out of control. A warning to those who aspire to office or to leadership is presented in Titus, where a bishop is described as one who is master of self, upright, holy, and *self-controlled*. What stories could be told about how the mighty have fallen, how men have lost control of their lives, how they turned over control of their future to inner forces they could not control. How weak we are, we who pretend to have all the parts of our life together.

II. But God Has Everything Under Control

Only God can overcome those powers "out there" that seek to take charge of us. He does it by dwelling "inside" us to transform us from within.

A. God's Rule Was Displayed

The person who is the center and occasion of the power struggle in our world is not even presented in the words of today's text. But He is not far away. He is always present in human lives. Peter forgot how close He was, even *who* He was, in his rush to dissociate himself from Him that day. No one chose to be "with Jesus of Nazareth." Jesus had to go it alone. But Jesus had Himself and His world always under His control because He had handed over control of His life to His Father. Peter forgot Jesus, in more ways than one: he neglected and denied Him and then ran away from Him, perhaps more subtly but every bit as certainly as the other disciples did. Jesus remembered Peter. It was for Peter and all of us like him that Jesus controlled His actions and refused to turn aside from His path to the cross. He would not abandon us, who so quickly turn aside from Him. He would not deny His saving desire and obligation to help Peter and us, who automatically consign Him and everything about Him to the chaos that threatens to emerge as the champion. Jesus is not mentioned in the text, just as He was not seen as God in the flesh by many who chose to look elsewhere or to close their eyes to Him. But He was the Man for all to look at and admire for His self-control. He pulled together by His own strength and subdued by His own weakness all the elements of life that seem uncontrolled. In His lonely torment He assumed the chaos of life and sank into it, passing from cross to grave without a word of cursing or commotion. He did not and could not deny His orientation: He is with God and God is with Him.

B. God Has Resumed Control of the World

Many of us have driven cars with cruise control mechanisms that allow the driver to maintain an established speed. Acceleration and braking that normally are required to speed up or slow down the car are programmed automatically. In special circumstances the driver may override or disconnect that control to take direct charge of the vehicle. God did that in the world that He had made and set to running. In Jesus Christ He took direct control and dealt with the need to overcome the dangers of life. And once raised from the dead, Jesus Christ is Lord. God "pushed the button" on the world's cruise control as planet earth moved on. God was able to *resume* control of people's lives, as He had originally planned, through Jesus Christ. At the close of today's text we see Peter getting his life under control again. The first step is to remember Jesus and His words. In the tumult of life Jesus restores order and brings meaning out of confusion.

God does not deny His created world. He redeems it. The world is a good world, and God has a good plan for it. That goal is frustrated and goes out of control, however, unless God stays involved. Christians need not and cannot abandon the world either, despite the chaos and confusion that characterize it. God's Spirit does not lead us to asceticism so that we resort to running off to some safe place where we cannot be confronted with danger. God's Spirit moves us toward total sanctification, where more of life and existence are under His control. Jesus does not call people to deny the created world but to deny *themselves* and to be controlled by God. Every day we face the threats to our identity that threatened Peter. Each day we can begin again to put our lives under God's control. In the terms of Luther's *Small Catechism,* each day we drown the sin in us and put on the Lord Jesus Christ. Each day His Spirit takes control of us again.

Paul recognized the need to control his human body just as he acknowledged that "every athlete exercises self-control in all things." He also recognized the legitimate needs of body and emotions. In marriage, Paul said, one must neither over-control nor fail to control the sexual impulse, but must place it under the control of God's Spirit. He directs Christians to marry if they cannot exercise self-control. St. James speaks to another aspect of human life that requires self-control, namely, the tongue and our speech. Peter's accent and speech betrayed him to the bystanders and led them to draw conclusions and make statements about his identification with Jesus. Our use of the tongue identifies us as people with Jesus too. James admits that no person can by himself control his tongue, but the gift of God's Spirit and the fruit of Jesus' redemption are able to grace our speech.

Jesus fulfilled all the laws given to the Jews, as we read in Paul's letter to the Galatians, "For the whole law is fulfilled in one word, 'You shall love your neighbor as yourself.'" Paul further shows by his words on self-control that Jesus grants to those who believe in Him the completion and embodiment of all that Greek idealism had sought as well. Jesus is the perfect Man, self-assured yet divinely-controlled, divinely-assured and therefore *self-controlled.* The power of Jesus' redemption is so great that we who are one with Him share in His Spirit and benefits. Self-control is the final term in the list of the fruit of the Spirit in Gal. 5:22, and Paul concludes, "Against such there is no law." God's Spirit is the signal from God to which we respond, as a receiver is activated by remote control, for our words and actions. From the distance of heaven and in the midst of life, God tunes Himself to our frequency and controls our lives so that we move in ways that are pleasing to Him.

Conclusion

At times the chaos that surrounds our lives drives us in desperation to seek escape in oblivion and forgetfulness. In Ephesians Paul turns God's people from alcohol spirits and other diversions to the power of God: "Do not get drunk with wine," he says, "but be filled with the Spirit." When we are "under the influence" of God's good Spirit, we will be moved to give Him thanks in the name of our Lord Jesus Christ. God's Spirit is the control that we need to deal with the pressures of daily living and the threats to good order that confuse us. Jesus has taken us to the Leader, to the one, only God, from whom and to whom and through whom are all things. We may weep bitterly (with Peter) at our weakness, but we shall emerge from the darkness transformed. We live by the power of that Spirit who gives us self-control. We can do better than Peter did in the courtyard because the risen Christ blesses us with the fruit of self-control.

Lent 6

Peace from the Passion of Christ

Matt. 27:11-24

Introduction

Pontius Pilate had a personal problem. He was perplexed and puzzled. He was confronted with Christ in a situation that defied solution. Neither logic nor emotion seemed to provide the answer. What was he to do with this Man who stood before him? How had all these events conspired to put him in this awkward position? What would he do? What could he do? His mind raced back and forth over the possibilites as he tried to fit the pieces together. But one piece was missing. In fact, what was missing was PEACE itself: peace of mind, peace of soul—call it what you will, Pilate did not have peace. There was a deep conflict within his heart because he was not at peace with God. His life was disturbed.

I. Jesus Disturbs People

Peace is harmony. As in a piece of music, real peace in life comes when all the separate and discordant elements blend into a complete whole. We want that peace. Sometimes we are ready for "peace at any price." We are too ready to make peace with whatever troubles us, even on the wrong terms. And then there can be no peace, despite our best efforts and sincerest wishes.

A. People (Like Pilate) Don't Have Peace

God won't let people make their own peace, on their own terms. Jesus warned that He did not come to bring peace to people who wanted an easy peace in this world. He came with a sword, as He says in Matthew's gospel, to cut people loose from their deceptive entrapment to quick solutions. It is not easy to correct people who have made up their minds to dictate peace on their terms. Jesus destroyed the illusion of simple question-and-answer solutions that people develop in order to provide a measure of peace for themselves. Pilate was full of questions. In general he must have asked: "Who is this Jesus? Why is He silent? Why is He second to Barabbas in the people's choice? Why are the religious leaders against Him? What has He done?" More personally he wondered: "Why is my wife so upset about this stranger? How could she know anything about Him?" Ultimately he pondered: "Why must Jesus die? Why the shouts to crucify Him? What has He done?" Many questions. But no satisfactory answers.

The answers that came easily to Pilate's mind weren't satisfactory answers. The leaders were envious. There was jealousy, professional rivalry, bad feeling between religious men. Someone feared competition. Jesus was a troublemaker. He was a threat to the *status quo*. He was changing too much, too fast, too soon. But still, "Why?" His wife had an answer, "My dream was a warning." Pilate wondered. A warning from whom? How? A warning of what? Perhaps Pilate knew about Joseph, son of Jacob, "the dreamer," from the pages of God's book. Did that knowledge help? Had he ever heard about the other Joseph, husband of Mary, who was told in a dream about this Jesus who now confronted Pilate? Can one *dream* the truth? Pilate scoffed. "What is truth?" he questioned Jesus. The people, always vocal but seldom profound, had their answers. They needed a scapegoat. Doesn't everyone? There was evil abroad when this Jesus came. But did He cause it? Or did He just suffer it? Pilate didn't know. He had no peace. No one could under the circumstances.

B. People Today Are Without Peace

Pilate is the model of the modern man. He is no ancient storybook figure. Pilate is a reflection of most of humankind. People today seek peace and good days, but they can't find it. People don't know how to be at peace. They manifest the same symptoms that were present in this first-century scene: wrath and fighting and disquiet and anxiety. People shout claims and counterclaims. Mouths are open: lives are empty. Nobody has true peace. Everyone is afraid. In quiet times the world is "waiting for the other shoe to drop." Almost afraid to breathe, people hold their collective breath and say, "Peace and safety." Maybe (they hope) just saying the words can make it happen. Maybe the dream speaks reality. Perhaps the wish can come true. Not so. According to 1 Thessalonians, "When people say, 'There is peace and security,' then sudden destruction will come upon them."

There is no peace without the Prince of Peace. But people want to wash their hands of Him, and be done with Him, and move on to other more urgent tasks which hold the illusion of contentment and peace. Pilate washed his hands before the people's sight, but water was not enough. The people wanted to "wash" their hands in Jesus' blood, but not to make peace with God.

II. Jesus Gives Peace to Troubled People

How then can people find any peace? By a complete reversal. Peace must find us. Peace comes from God toward us in the person and power of Jesus. And Jesus will not rest; *He* will have no peace until peace comes to all people on earth.

A. Peace Can Come to People Today

Christ comes today with a peace "which the world cannot give" and offers a way for us to live "in rest and quietness," as a traditional collect phrases it. He is the proof that peace cannot be imposed by force or might, as military men and eager empires have attempted to do. All the force of arms and any ultimate-weapon dependency only escalate hostilities. Peace cannot be created by the minds and thoughts of men. In contradiction of the theme of the 1965 World's Fair in New York, there is no "peace through understanding." Knowledge and logic and reasoning and answers do not result in peace. They only create more questions. Peace is always GIVEN. It is the gift of God. He promises peace and He delivers it.

Jews speak of *shalom,* that state of well-being that assures God's care and keeping as defined by God's covenant with Israel in old days. God promised to establish peace with His people. He would create peace, and He would maintain it. God also provided peace for His people. He guaranteed it and He restored it. *God's* answers and thoughts and dreams and logic mean peace for all, although some may not rest easy with His grace. St. Paul knew and believed in the reality of God's peace. He received it and proclaimed: "We *have* peace with God." "*Let us have* peace with God" from the bottom of our hearts because God has placed it there. Edmund Brown says that "peace is the quiet, calm assurance that God is with me and will guide and love me always, and always invites me to rely upon Him." Paul was given that peace, and God gives it to us too.

B. Peace Proceeds from Pilate's Praetorium

Unsought and unwelcome, God's peace came to humankind. Return to the opening scene. Pilate is not at peace, nor the people, nor their leaders. Where could one find peace in the confusion and horror of suffering and death? Look to Jesus. There is peace. Peace is embodied in the man Jesus, who stands boldly before all. In Jerusalem, "Salem-city," the city of peace as it is named, the paradox is unveiled: the city that Jesus said "didn't know the things that make for peace" had peace brought into her in the person of Jesus as God-making-peace-with-people.

Humankind's prayer for peace is answered by Jesus. Zacharias, the man who asked God to "guide our feet in the way of peace," had a son who pointed out the path that leads to Jesus. When Jesus was born, the angels sang of "heavenly peace." But the peace was not dramatically and predominately "peace on earth," as St. Luke emphasizes. On earth, peace. In Pilate's palace, peace. Right before his eyes, peace. Why couldn't he see that? Because he needed God's Spirit to produce peace in him. Jesus was at peace with God, His Father, and so He could "hold His peace" when warring factions accused Him. Jesus is *our* peace, as Paul's Epistle to the Ephesians repeats, and He destroys all the walls that we may still build to keep peace for ourselves by keeping others out. Jesus' blood, which the Jews claimed and Pilate avoided, is the peace-making blood that establishes the new covenant of peace for God and man. By the blood of Christ, the war between the holy God and sinful humankind has come to an end. The contest of wills between the Lord and people is resolved when Jesus imposes peace by His cross. He is the Mediator between Creator and creature. He grants forgiveness. He puts together His blood and His body in the Holy Sacrament and we receive Him and His peace in the bread and wine. Peace is found in the kingdom of God, not in the empire of Romans (or Jews). Jesus

93

is the Lord and Center of that Kingdom. His Spirit, given after He rose from the dead, characterizes Christian existence as being "eager to maintain the unity of the Spirit in the bond of peace."

Before His death Jesus had explained: "I leave you peace, but it is more than the world's peace, and so you need not fear." After His death, He rose and confronted His fearful flock with His word: "Peace I bring to you." Peace is now given by Jesus. We receive His Spirit in our baptism, and by faith we are attached to that Prince of Peace from whom we inherit total peace.

Conclusion

Jesus gives us His peace so that we may share it. His people "pass the peace" to others in their worship and their life-circle. The gift of peace is kept by giving it to others. In the liturgy of sanctuary and of world, we find the solution to our life-puzzles to be the centerpiece of our life, Jesus, our peace. His peace passes our understanding and guards us daily. Daily we grow and live in His peace. The early church "had peace and was built up," according to the summary report in the book of Acts, and the same is true of Christ's church today. Each of us in Christ is given the power to live with others and to answer life's questions on the basis of His peacemaking effort. In Him all the discordant parts of our lives fit together. We live and work in peace. We can even die in peace. And finally we "rest in peace"—because we rest in the Lord.

Maundy Thursday

Kindness from the Passion of Christ
Matt. 26:26-29

Introduction

This is a holy week. And we are God's holy people. We are approaching the time that commemorates the crucifixion of the holy Son of God. We pray that we may be holy as He is holy, dedicated to God in all of life. When St. Paul speaks of the fruit of the Spirit in Galatians 5:22, he indicates that the grace and power of God daily produce the responses He desires. We are conformed to Christ and possess those qualities that mark Him in His Passion. Today we again join together Spirit-fruit and Passion-Story, comparing the Gospel account of Jesus and His disciples at the Last Supper with the fruit of *kindness.*

We live in an impersonal business-oriented society. Our modern method of electronically recorded and automatically transferred financial transactions illustrates that we deal in nontangible values. Our day-to-day financial dealings are also abstract. In most cases we have left behind the ancient bartering or trading systems which dealt in tangibles and physical goods. We seldom talk about payment in kind, and yet that type of transaction has a more permanent and deeper value in many ways. Which is better and more "human," giving (or receiving) that is computerized, distant, and impersonal? Or the exchange of something that is physically present? For example, if a hungry person asked you for help, which would be more valuable for both parties: a few dollars to "go and buy something?" Or a handmade sandwich and personally prepared lunch? What does each type of transaction say about the relationship of the people involved?

I. Jesus Expressed His Kindness

Jesus never dealt impersonally with people. He wasn't distant from them or far removed from their needs. His familiarity may be hard for some people to swallow, like taking a gulp of some strong drink. Jesus always was personally kind and good to those He helped. His was a very personal, "hands-on" kind of helping.

A. He Shared with His Disciples

Perhaps some people appeared on the scene who longed for the milk of

95

human kindness, like the milk a baby wants. Jesus had a kind word for them. He nourished them. And they, in the words of 1 Peter, tasted the kindness of the Lord. Jesus could encourage people to "taste and see that the Lord is good." Some people may have been reluctant to sample new tastes. After all, everyone tends to agree with the opinion that "old wine" is better. So why change? At the wedding in Cana the man in charge of provisions was surprised to find that the better-tasting wine was not served earlier. Jesus offered a "new wine" which was pleasing to the tastes of all people. And that's how we were saved when we were served with Jesus. In the sight and sound and feel of those who were with Jesus, "the goodness and loving-kindness of God our Savior *appeared.*" So Paul states in his letter to Titus. Notice that God's kingdom *appeared*: God was present, and He could be experienced as a reality and not as an abstraction. Of course, some people took advantage of God's generosity in His handout. (Some people inevitably confuse kindness with weakness.) Nevertheless, Jesus did not draw back from grasping hands and did not hold back from selfish seekers. He drank the cup of God's wrath that no human could swallow. He walked alone in the winepress where "the grapes of wrath" were stored. He became the prodigal Son who showered the Father's wealth in all directions and did not ration His kindness. God's vintage was wrapped in Jesus' human skin. God doled out His wealth on the cross in preparation for the day when His gifts could be freely served to all. Jesus picked up the check and signed His name on our tab so that God would see our bill paid in full and free us from the burden of satisfying our obligation to Him.

On Maundy Thursday Jesus and His disciples sat at table together for the last time during His earthly ministry. But the ferment that He had caused in the world during His brief lifetime continued even after His death. After His death on the cross, the pressure of God's Spirit forced open the grave where He had been buried like a host popping the cork on a bottle of champagne. Then the celebration began, for Jesus rose from the dead. The living water of God's Spirit could flow freely from Jesus to His people.

B. The Ascended Lord Shares with Us in His Kingdom

We today celebrate how God showed His kindness toward us and all people in Christ. It is as if we were already seated with Christ at the victory banquet in the heavenly places. Jesus vowed it to His disciples: He would eat and drink again in the Kingdom, with them and now with all who accept His invitation. The private stock that He has in reserve for us is preserved in a storehouse of forgiveness. We receive kindness and forgiveness from Him in order to share it freely and gladly with one another. Paul exhorts, "Be *kind* to one another, tenderhearted, forgiving one another, as God in Christ forgave you."

In this meal we feast together with the disciples and the saints of all time, united in happiness and gladness. God has grafted us into the vine of Israel, Paul says in Romans, and that is abundant kindness! We echo the praise of the psalmist, "O how abundant is Thy *goodness,* which Thou has laid up for those who fear Thee." To be at such a feast is a moving experience. Drinking His wine is truly heartwarming. His wine brings warmth to our body and even tears to our eyes as we gulp it down to satisfy our great thirst. Feel it coming into your mouth. Swish it around. Enjoy the delicate bouquet. Let Christ's blood-wine slowly trickle down your throat. Savor every drop, for it is Jesus who is present. He is able to save and to serve and is now to be served to us too.

II. So We Can Be His Kind of People

Such heavenly drink is very heady. Our natural inhibitions and controlled behavior may be loosened by our eating and drinking with our Lord. This kind of refreshment may lead us to respond *in kindness*. It is not easy or natural to show kindness, especially to strangers and undesirables. In this area certainly we are often open to indictment, for we have not done good or been kind; no one does *good*, not even one, says the Scripture. But we are now especially motivated by God's kindness, to give thanks in the sight of others and for their benefit. His Spirit, in Sacrament as in Word, fills us with kindness to share with others.

A. First We Receive His Kindness

Jesus speaks to us about His kind of love when He says in verse 28, "This is My blood of the covenant, which is poured out for many for the forgiveness of sins." His style and manner are kind, matching His speech. He does not use "fair and flattering" words to deceive us. What He presents is true love and sincere kindness. He gives Himself to us. That is easy to swallow. Kindness is the yoke which ties us together with Him, and when He is so near and so good, His "yoke is easy," as He promises us. We "old wineskins" cannot contain the new wine of kindness without bursting, but He is with us to repair us and to replace what we lose. We become a new kind of human and heavenly receptacle, a dispenser of the kindness of God which He has lavished upon us. God's kindness spills out on all sides of us, and yet not a drop is lost.

B. Then We Show Kindness as He Does

God's plan for human reproduction in Genesis applies also to the reproduction of kindness with others in the New Testament era. When we are "fruitful and multiply," each produces "after its own *kind*." God's Spirit makes us like Jesus, and our kindness duplicates His in manner if not in size. Jesus (on the night we call Maundy Thursday) gave the disciples His love in a special kind of serving of eternal food at His table. Then He commanded them, "Love one another as I have loved you." What great love for us—that we can receive and then emulate His kindness. Love is patient and *kind*, and love is all forgiving too. Love received from Christ is love that transforms a person into a model of kindness like the Master. Luther describes the Christian as a person with "a gentleness and sweetness in manner and in one's entire life. For Christians should not be harsh and morose; they should be gentle, humane, affable, courteous, people with whom others enjoy associating, people who overlook the mistakes of others or put the best construction on them, people who willingly yield to others, who bear with the recalcitrant" (*Luther's Works,* vol. 27, p. 94). Jesus says that God is kind to the ungrateful and to the selfish. So we can love our enemies. Paul, in his list of Christian qualities in 2 Corinthians, decribes kindness as essential to Christian disposition. It is true and possible for us to be that kind because God's Spirit produces kindness in us.

Conclusion

In the history of the church, differences of practice and in teaching have not always been resolved with kindness. Ironically, one of the doctrinal arguments in Christian history had to do with the mode of Communion, whether Christians receive the bread only or receive both bread and wine. The latter is called "communing under both *kinds*." As long as the Eucharist is used for debate and discussion, acrimony and disagreement will prevail. The elements are, as it were, placed on the back of the shelf, while the controversy rages and the doctrinal issue is on the table. But when God's people receive the bread and wine, a firsthand confrontation with God's kindness overcomes the hatred that disagreements arouse. Holy Communion is for nourishment rather than debate.

In this holy meal Christ gives us Himself. We have wine for celebration and bread for sustenance. In, with, and under both kinds He is really present, to strengthen us for life and death. We receive the power of His blood, and so we benefit because His body is formed within us. The simple prayer of a child is appropriate at the Holy Communion: "Lord, make the bad people good and the good people nice." We can be nice when we share Christ's kindness. Having a God of love whose kindness we experience so tangibly and realistically in the Lord's Supper can do miracles in us. Our Lord is a God who is good to all. We too can be that kind.

Good Friday

Love from the Passion of Christ

Mark 15:33-39

Introduction

What a tragedy when there is unrequited love. When love is a one-sided experience, when the other person doesn't "love back," great heartaches and sadness are the results. Unrequited love suggests to us individually what we suspect all along: they don't love us because we aren't lovable. The poets say loves makes the world go 'round, but it is easier to say the word than it is to know true love. It is harder still to do. Love is a scarce item in this world. But without clear and certain proof of another's love, unrequited love dies.

I. Love Is Hard to See in This World

To Christians, the cross is a symbol of love. On the cross where Jesus died, we say God's love was made manifest. But when we look at the cross without that faith present to define it, the cross is obscured by the darkness of nonlove and judgment.

A. Jesus Died "in the Dark"

Jesus' cry from the cross expresses the fact that darkness had enveloped Him. He was forsaken by God. Jesus' cry, and His personal anguish indicate the depths of damnation that He was experiencing. Despite His call for care and love, Jesus received no satisfaction. His Father gave no answer when He cried out. The spectator nearby gave Him no sympathy or understanding. What a disappointment and challenge to faith: can this be God's *beloved* Son, as He was called at His baptism? A Father has a strange kind of love if He abandons His child in His darkest hour and refuses to help or even to answer Him. A love that gives no light or warmth in the darkness and cold of the world is no love at all, as we see it.

B. Men Still Love Darkness

The scene at the cross is really little different from the way the claim of love is tested now and always has been challenged in the world. Today or yesterday, anyday and everyday, darkness tries to overcome light. No one wants to be always "an instrument of peace" for God. It is unusual for a person to pray, "Where there is hatred, let me sow love," with any degree of sincerity. Instead hatred breeds hatred, and pain is added to pain. As then, so now, there is the added torment of mockery and torture. "He wants a drink?" someone asks. "Give Him vinegar!" There is no help available, only added torment. When someone is hurting and on the way down, ignore him. Or taunt him. Make fun of him, for there's so little pleasure to be found anywhere. Don't help. "Wait," they say. "Let's enjoy this awhile." Jesus had been derided earlier according to the verses immediately preceeding today's text. By this time all the jokes and humor were getting old. "Just ignore Him." It makes no difference who does what. Close your eyes to the pain and your ears to the wailing. People don't see, or don't want to see, ways to help. We too won't find ways to help, and we excuse ourselves by saying we *can't* help. We are overwhelmed by the challenge. We are bored by the sameness. We are dulled by the monotony. We are blinded by the darkness. Our ears barely catch His reaction. What is He saying? "Father, forgive them. They don't know...," Who knows what that means? Who sees any sense in the words of a dying man? Humor Him, if you must. Use Him, as you will. It makes no difference. Nobody sees any glimmer of hope anywhere. It's as dark now as it was then. There was darkness at the cross. There always is.

II. God's Love Is Clearly Seen

Maybe we're too close to the cross, for the moment. If Christ on the cross is too familiar for us, like the details on the face of our watch, the actions of God can easily be overlooked. Mark, the writer of the gospel to the *Gentiles,* points out how distance and perspective can give new and true insights into meaninglessness and obscurity. Mark pictures the Gentile centurion facing the man on the cross. He saw and he confessed what he saw: "Son of God." God's Spirit led him to a faith and confession not experienced by many others.

A. We Can See How Much He Loves Us

Eyes can be opened when they look simply and honestly at the Man on the cross. Vision is clear when it is "cross-eyed." The sight and vision of faith occurs when God opens eyes to pierce the darkness. How could we see God's love when a dark curtain is before our eyes? But the curtain between God and people, which separated them for their mutual protection, has been torn down the middle. Now Jesus is in the middle in place of the covering veil. He is between God and us. Love sees Him in the dark and responds to the touch of the Beloved. God and His people see each other and are seen by one another. There is nothing hidden now, but the reality is clear: God put Jesus on the cross, FOR ME. I put Jesus on the cross, FOR MY SINS. The report of His death is not simply history, the tracing of a line through the ages. Death (and resurrection) are HIS story, His story and MINE. I have not loved, but He has loved me. I have been buried with Christ and raised with Him. Jesus was unloved at the cross because God gave all His love *to me* at the cross. Jesus is the Son of God *for me.* Here, in His dying, I am being loved to death—and to life.

B. We Can See Where to Give Our Love

With that much love coming to me, I have all the love I need—and more. I am loved so much that I have love to spare, love to give. My faith works by love, as Paul teaches in Galatians; love actualizes itself in the giving and helping that are the marks of Jesus' love. We are reminded in Scripture of God's command to "love your neighbor." And the neighbor is the one we see to be suffering and in need. And then, in mysterious fashion, the neighbor and Jesus merge and become one. Jesus is the least of His brothers. He says, "As you did it to one of the least of these My brethren, you did it to Me." We love Him by loving them.

His love covered our sins, and so our love covers their sins. "Truly, love covers a multitude of sins," says 1 Peter. His love met our needs. Our love meets theirs. He was the one forsaken, and He is suffering and calling for help today. I can hear *them;* I can see *them.* When I see and hear them, I see and hear HIM. In His death Jesus breathed out His spirit, the last act of a dying man. And breathing out His Spirit is also the first act of a life-giving man. It is the power of the Lord who is the Spirit. He breathed out His Spirit on us, His church, and He breathed His Spirit into us, His body on earth. Wherever His people are at work in Him name, there love can be seen in the world. St. Paul was a famous man who was commended to his congregation on the basis of his special gifts and service. But he was commended to them all the more by love, which is the culmination of all virtues. Paul could exhort his readers and listeners to be agents of God's love and bearers of His Spirit: "I appeal to you, brethren, by our Lord Jesus Christ and by the *love* of the Spirit, to strive together with me in your prayers to God on my behalf." Love caused him and them and us and others to see that there is pardon, where there is injury; that there is faith, where there is doubt; that there is hope, where there is despair; that *there is light, where there is darkness;* that there is joy, where there is sadness.

The world needs love, wherever there are people. Where the people of God are, love is present for those in need.

Conclusion

So don't leave others "in the dark" about the love of God. Don't let anyone in the world imagine that the darkness will overcome the light, for St. John says, "The light shines in the darkness, and the darkness has not overcome it." Children can teach adults about the "Gospel-light" and how it is to shine. Adults can show children by word and example that love does not have to be unrequited and one-sided. Paul was pleased and comforted to hear from co-worker Epaphras about the Colossians' "love of the Spirit," and he commended them for it. It is always refreshing and satisfying to see love among others, especially when there is enough love close enough for us to feel loved, too. The world's subsitiues for real and genuine love will not prevail or keep it going 'round. Genuine love, according to Paul's definition, means to "hate that which is evil, hold fast to that which is good." Two-way love, with both God and people acting in love toward one another, creates a continuing love relationship: God loves me; I love God. God loves you; and I love you too. Only one element remains incomplete: love me too, as you love God.

Easter

Joy from the Passion of Christ

John 20:11-18

Introduction

The joyful Easter statement "He is risen!" means nothing if you don't know that Jesus was buried. To know that "Jesus is alive!" provokes little reaction unless you realize that He was dead. To preach and proclaim the message of Easter to people who haven't heard what preceded the Resurrection is like telling the punch line of a joke without the previous setup. Some people come to Easter like a theater-goer arriving for the last three minutes of the movie, who then complain that the story doesn't make sense and wonder why it doesn't mean much to them. To look at the last chapter of a mystery novel and discover that "the butler did it" is not a totally satisfying experience. There has to be something of preparation in advance of the final word.

During the weeks of Lent this year we have again been considering the events in the closing days of Jesus' ministry on earth. At the same time we have seen how our Savior transfers to us the power to live our Christian lives by conveying His Spirit to us. We have been linking the "fruit of the Spirit" listed in Galatians 5:22 to various episodes in Jesus' Passion, and we are prepared today to participate in the celebration of Resurrection-*joy*. For joy is the gift of God and fruit of the Spirit. Joy is our response to the Good News about Jesus that comes to us today. Easter declares to us that we come to life only as we pass through what the psalmist calls "the valley of the shadow of death" or, as the *Good News Bible* translates, "the deepest darkness." Only then can we honestly claim to "fear no evil." Only then do we have joy.

I. The Experience of Death Separates People

It's not easy to come face-to-face with the grave. But it's more natural to do so when a person is already bent over with grief and looking down to the ground. That's the position Mary was in on the first Easter morning, when she came to Jesus' tomb.

A. Sorrow Speaks of Not Knowing

Mary wanted to take care of her dear, departed loved one. She came to the grave with sorrow but also with honor and respect for the dead. Like the other Mary depicted in the statue called the *Pieta,* she wanted to embrace and care for the lifeless body of Jesus. What good would that do? What would it change? In fact, it would probably change nothing, but how else could she respond to a loved one's death? The loss and absence of someone who is close causes such confusion and shock that a person can hardly be faulted for not acting rationally. Jesus had died. Jesus was dead. Jesus died. Jesus was not alive. Her mind knew that, but the human mind cannot really comprehend the truth of death in just a few days. In fact, the experiences of the past few days had only sharpened the memory of Jesus' life. Mary remembered so much: what He had said, what He had done, the Person He was, their time together. And then came also the recollection of His final hours: the private gathering with "His own" in the Upper Room, the prayer in Gethsemane, the arrest, the trial, the gradual realization by all those involved that there would be no escape for Him. The disciples had a few glimpses of Him, a few later reports of what had taken place. Clear in Mary's mind, now numbed at the horror of recalling it, was His pitiable appearance on the march out of town. And worst of all, she remembered the hours He had hung before them on the cross. The pain. The agony. The few mumbled words. The unending ignorance and cruelty of the bystanders, even while He was breathing His last. The shout. The gasp. The breath. And then: the silence. The silence of death. Jesus was dead! The writer to the Hebrews describes Jesus as the One "who for the joy that was set before Him endured the cross." The ultimate joy that Jesus anticipated had been punctuated and delayed by the reality of the agony of the cross.

B. All the World Knows the Answers

It's not customary for someone to ask at a graveside, "Why are you weeping?" Everyone knows the answer to that question. The bereaved are weeping because there's nothing else they can do. The survivors weep because they alone survive. Those left behind must weep because they have been left behind. Weeping won't change anything, but it's wise to say, "Go ahead and cry. Get it out of your system." That's good therapy. It's necessary to cry. It's good to cry. It's all right to cry. It won't change anything, but crying isn't meant to *change* anything. Weeping is just part of the process of dealing with death, or perhaps of avoiding the feel of death. Tears can blind one to what is happening and keep a person from seeing the horror of death. No matter that we may not recognize those around us because of tears in our eyes. They can't help anyway. In death, we are isolated. Everyone knows it, "Weep, and you weep alone." But who could be so unknowing, so insensitive to the raw emotion exposed in reaction to death, as to ask the question in the text, "Why are you weeping?" Only someone who doesn't understand what the world knows, that death ends it all. Isn't it obvious? Death separates, death wins, death is lord, death is the great teacher. The lesson is painful to learn, but everyone knows it's true: dead is dead. Everyone in the world weeps at personally learning that truth.

II. Jesus Reversed Death and Brought Joy to Life

But who is really Lord and Teacher? Who is *my* Lord? Who is my *Teacher?* It is Jesus, not the world. On Ash Wednesday, when we heard the foot-washing account, the disciples recognized Jesus as Lord and Teacher, even though He was underfoot to cleanse the disciples. He is here again now. He is still here, to teach and to rule me, as He has been with me from the start. In His Passion and resurrection Jesus has been in charge and leading me.

A. Listen to What He Says

Jesus is alive! He is here, now. He is speaking to me. He is casting out the sorrow that death always brings to me. He said that what He spoke would put His joy in His hearers so that they would be *full* of joy. Later He prayed for His disciples," ... that they may have my joy fulfilled in themselves." And now He is here and He is speaking to me. As I mourn for death as I have felt it, I am like Mary this morning. All He said to her was, "Mary." One word. Just her name. But one word says it all, especially if it is my name too. Jesus promises that then "your sorrow will turn into joy." And He goes on to promise that "I will see you again and your hearts will rejoice, and no one will take your joy from you." Luther says of Jesus' address: "This is the voice of the Bridegroom and the bride; it means joyful thoughts about Christ, wholesome exhortations, happy songs, praise, and thanksgiving, with which godly people exhort, arouse, and refresh one another. Therefore God is repelled by sorrow of spirit. He hates sorrowful teaching and sorrowful thoughts and words, and He takes pleasure in happiness. For He came to refresh us, not to sadden us" (*Luther's Works,* vol. 27, p. 93).

He is alive now! "Where?" we ask. It's all right to ask, because by receiving the answer, Jesus says *"our* joy will be full." It was good for Mary that she was able to see and hear Him, we might think, but what about us who live centuries after? We can rejoice too because Jesus is still alive, centuries after the morning when He called Mary's name. He has called me by name too. And so even though we do not see Him in the way that Mary did, we believe in Him and rejoice with "unutterable and exalted joy." After His word to Mary He ascended to His Father, and His Father is *my* Father. He ascended to God, to *our* God. In the God who is Spirit, Jesus new-creates joy at each recollection and sharing of His Easter-life. When I was lost in sorrow and grief, or others were, He found all of us who were lost and brought joy in the household of faith. The temporary pain of separation and loss has been turned into the permanent joy of gain and eternal union. God's discipline teaches us what Jesus learned. It is through trials—even when death separates us—that God sets us free. So you can "count it all joy ... when you meet various trials" because the Lord is your Teacher. And your Teacher rules all things.

B. Speak of What You Have Heard

Mary had to let loose of Jesus. He said that He would ascend and return in the Spirit to all His people. But "loose" does not mean "lose." And giving does not mean losing. Sharing the Word and the life of Christ rather means gain for all, speaker and hearer. Mary took, the report of her Easter experience first to His brothers. "Believe it or not," she said, "I have seen the Lord!" And believe it or not, *I* tell you today, "I have seen the Lord." So I rejoice with great joy too. Many were given joy at the birth of John the Baptizer, as his father Zechariah was promised. The angel said, "And you will have *joy* and gladness, and many will rejoice at his birth." But the greater and the best joy came to that prophet and baptizer when John knew the joy of welcoming Christ. It is John the Baptizer, according to Scripture, who *"rejoices* greatly at the bridegroom's voice; therefore this *joy* of mine is now full." Luke surrounds this gospel report of Jesus' life and work with the true joy, for the new life which the Spirit gives cannot be lived except in joy. From start to finish Luke speaks of joy. At the birth of Jesus there was joy. The word of the angels was, "I bring you Good News of a great *joy* which will come to all the people." Even when Jesus had ascended to heaven Luke records that the disciples "returned to Jerusalem with *joy.*" Such joy is for *all* people, and many believers in the early church felt repeated *joy* as more believers were added to their number. Philip went to a city of Samaria and "so there was much *joy* in that city," it is reported in Acts. Acts also reports that Paul and Barnabas likewise "gave great *joy* to all the brethren" as they reported Gentile conversions.

Conclusion

We rejoice today because we can be together to celebrate the resurrection of Jesus for us. In the words of Paul to the Philippians, "Rejoice in the Lord always; again I will say, Rejoice." Joy is always for sharing with others. Death may isolate, but joy joins. Taking a cue from John's epistle, I say that it is a joy to be with people like you now and to tell you, "Christ is risen!" We share that joy face-to-face as Scripture encourages us to do. Paul exhorts us, "Complete my joy by being of the same mind, having the same love, being in full accord and of one mind." Where joy is fading or incomplete today, we pray that "the God of peace will fill you with all joy and peace in believing so that you may abound in hope." Some of us are near to death now. All of us must face death again tomorrow. But today we know that the Jesus who was dead is alive now. He speaks to us, and He is with us. His Spirit is in us and grants us His joy. Give thanks to God for the fruit of the Spirit that is joy. And rejoice: Christ is risen!

Part III:
Worship Resources
by Richard Kapfer

Gentleness from the Passion of Christ

The Call to Worship

P: The seasons change, winter to spring; and the daylight hours lengthen with a scent of freshness and renewal in the air.

C: **It's Lent again, and we come, O Lord, wondering about its deeper dimensions of meaning for our lives. Help us to prepare for Easter, to discover signs of resurrection and to enrich the quality of our spiritual awareness in the 40 plus days ahead. Guide us as we explore significant aspects of the life, death, and resurrection of Jesus Christ. In His name we pray. Amen.**

The Hymn: "Jesus, I Will Ponder Now"

The Responsive Prayer

P: Father, the Lenten season is once more upon us. It is time to pause, watch, reflect, confess.

C: **It is time to be honest with ourselves and honest to God.**

P: It is time to watch the Man of Sorrows, the One acquainted with grief.

C: **"For surely He has borne our griefs and carried our sorrows; yet we esteemed Him stricken, smitten of God and afflicted.**

P: But He was wounded for our transgressions, He was bruised for our iniquities;

C: **Upon Him was the chastisement that made us whole, and with His stripes we are healed.**

P: All we like sheep have gone astray; we have turned every one to his own way;

C: **And the Lord has laid on Him the iniquity of us all.**

P: He was oppressed, and He was afflicted, yet He opened not His mouth;

C: **Like a lamb that is led to the slaughter—how like a lamb, the very Lamb of God who takes away the sin of the world!**

P: And like a sheep that before its shearers is dumb,

C: **So He opened not His mouth.**

P: By oppression and judgment He was taken away; and for His generation, who considered that He was cut off out of the land of the living,

C: **Stricken for the transgression of His people.**

P: And they made His grave with the wicked and with a rich man in His death,

C: **Although He had done no violence, and there was no deceit in His mouth."**

P: That is why Lent begins on this Ash Wednesday, with ashes of repentance

C: **And with the hope of life out of the ashes.**

P: With the Lord Jesus in His suffering, humiliation, agony, and bloody sweat;

C: **And at a cross where He took our sins upon Himself.**

P: That great exchange—God's mercy and forgiveness purchased at the cost of His own Son!

C: **"For God so loved the world that He gave His only-begotten Son, that whosoever believeth in Him should not perish, but have everlasting life." Amen.**

(Is. 53:4-9; John 3:16)

The Scripture Reading: John 13:1-17

The Sermon Hymn: "The Lord's My Shepherd, I'll Not Want"

The Ash Wednesday Message

Text: John 13:3-5 (1-17)

The Offering

The Offertory

All: **Let the vineyards be fruitful, Lord, and fill to the brim our cup of blessing. Gather a harvest from the seeds that were sown, that we may be fed with the bread of life. Gather the hopes and the dreams of all; unite them with the prayers we offer now. Grace our table with your presence, and give us a foretaste of the feast to come.**

The Ash Wednesday Litany on Gentleness

P: Put on then, as God's chosen ones, holy and beloved, compassion, kindness, lowliness, meekness, and patience, forbearing one another and, if one has a complaint against another, forgiving each other, as the Lord has forgiven you.

C: **Give to us the Spirit's gift of gentleness, O Lord.**

P: Lead a life worthy of the calling to which you have been called, with all lowliness and meekness, with patience, forbearing one another in love.

C: **Give to us the Spirit's gift of gentleness, O Lord.**

P: Always be prepared to make a defense to anyone who calls you to account for the hope that is in you; yet do it with gentleness and reverence.

C: **Give to us the Spirit's gift of gentleness, O Lord.**

P: If a man is overtaken in any trespass, you who are spiritual should restore him in a spirit of gentleness. Look to yourself, lest you too be tempted. Bear one another's burdens, and so fulfill the law of Christ.

C: Give to us the Spirit's gift of gentleness, O Lord.

P: Therefore put away all filthiness and rank growth of wickedness and receive with meekness the implanted Word, which is able to save your souls.

C: Give to us the Spirit's gift of gentleness, O Lord.

P: Who is wise and understanding among you? By his good life let him show his works in the meekness of wisdom.

C: Give to us the Spirit's gift of gentleness, O Lord.

(Col. 3:12; Eph. 4:1b-2; 1 Peter 3:15b; Gal. 6:1-2; James 1:21; 3:13)

The Confession of Sins

All: Forgive my sins, O Lord—Forgive me the sins of my present and the sins of my past, the sins of my soul and the sins of my body, the sins I have done to please myself and the sins I have done to please others. Forgive me my wanton and idle sins; forgive me my serious and deliberate sins; forgive me those sins which I know and those sins which I know not; forgive me the sins which I have labored so to hide from others that I have hid them from my own memory. Forgive them, O Lord; forgive them all. Of Your great mercy let me be absolved, and of Your bountiful goodness let me be delivered from the bonds of all that by my frailty I have committed. Grant this, O heavenly Father, for the sake of Jesus Christ, our blessed Lord and Savior. Amen.

P: Beloved in Christ, our Lord Jesus heard the prayer of our souls. He came to live among us. He stooped down to wash the feet of His disciples, taking upon Himself the task of a slave. He stooped down in order to be lifted up on a cross, taking upon Himself the sins of the world. His life is your life by faith. Your sins are forgiven. Now we do not need to be afraid to love. Amen.

The Lord's Prayer (All)

The Consecration

The Distribution of the Holy Communion

The Communion Hymns
"Chief of Sinners Though I Be"
"I Come, O Savior, to Your Table"

The Closing Collect

P: O God, by the patient suffering of Your only-begotten Son You have beaten down the pride of the old ememy. Now help us, we humbly pray, rightly to treasure in our hearts all that our Lord has of His goodness borne for our sake that after His example we may bear with patience all that is adverse to us; through Jesus Christ, our Lord.

C: Amen.

The Benediction

C: Amen.

The Closing Hymn: "Abide with Me"

Acknowledgments

"Let the vineyards be fruitful" from *Lutheran Book of Worship*, © 1978, CPH representing the publisher and copyright holders. Used by permission.

Unless otherwise indicated, Scripture references are from the Revised Standard Version of the Bible, copyrighted 1946, 1952 © 1971, 1973. Used by permission.

Copyright © 1984 Concordia Publishing House

Lent 2

Patience from the Passion of Christ

The Hymn of Invocation: "Savior, When in Dust to You"

The Opening Sentences

P: Lord, You are in the midst of us, and we are called by Your name:

C: Do not forsake us, O Lord our God.

P: Be pleased, O Lord, to deliver us:

C: O Lord, come quickly to help us.

All: Be present, O Holy Spirit, and bless this time set apart for You so that we, who are wearied by the changes and chances of this fleeting world, may rest upon Your eternal changelessness. Grant to each of us the fruit of patience, that we may trust Your loving will and be slow to anger and despair when life is not all we wish it to be. Fill us with hope through the sweet victory of Christ our Lord, in whose name we pray. Amen.

The Confession

P: Let us ask God's forgiveness for our sins and shortcomings this day.

All: Here and now, O Holy Lord, we bring our sins to You. We lie open in Your sight. We are sinful people, and through our own fault we have done wrong against You and others, in our actions and inaction. Be patient with us and forgive our sins, for the sake of our suffering Savior, Jesus Christ. Amen.

The Psalm of Absolution: Ps. 103:1-13 (adapted from TEV)

P: Praise the Lord, my soul! All my being, praise His holy name!

C: Praise the Lord, my soul, and do not forget how kind He is.

P: He forgives all my sins and heals all my diseases;

C: He saves me from the grave and blesses me with love and mercy.

P: He fills my life with good things, so that I stay young and strong like an eagle.

C: The Lord judges in favor of the oppressed and gives them their rights.

P: He told His plans to Moses and let the people of Israel see His mighty acts.

C: The Lord is merciful and loving, slow to become angry, and full of constant love.

P: He does not keep reprimanding; He is not angry forever.

C: **He does not punish us as we deserve or repay us for our sins and wrongs.**

P: As high as the sky is above the earth, so great is His love for those who fear Him.

C: **As far as the east is from the west, so far does He remove our sins from us.**

P: As kind as a father is to his children, so the Lord is kind to those who fear Him.

All: **Glory be to the Father and to the Son and to the Holy Spirit; as it was in in the beginning, is now, and will be for ever. Amen.**

The Scripture Reading: Mark 14:33-41

The Sermon Hymn: "Christ, the Life of All the Living"

The Sermon
Text: Matt. 26:36-46

The Offering

The Offertory Hymn: "Our God, Our Help in Ages Past"

The Litany on Patience

P: Abraham, having patiently endured, obtained the promise. And we desire each one of you to show the same earnestness in realizing the full assurance of hope until the end, so that you may not be sluggish, but imitators of those who through faith and patience inherit the promises.

C: **Produce in us the fruit of patience, O Holy Spirit.**

P: Be patient, therefore, brethren, until the coming of the Lord. Behold, the farmer waits for the precious fruit of the earth, being patient over it until it receives the early and the late rain. You also be patient.

C: **Produce in us the fruit of patience, O Holy Spirit.**

P: And we exhort you, brethren, admonish the idlers, encourage the faint-hearted, help the weak, be patient with them all. See that none of you repays evil for evil, but always seek to do good to one another and to all.

C: **Produce in us the fruit of patience, O Holy Spirit.**

P: May you be strengthened with all power, according to His glorious might, for all endurance and patience with joy, giving thanks to the Father who has qualified us to share in the inheritance of the saints in light.

C: **Produce in us the fruit of patience, O Holy Spirit.**

P: Lead a life worthy of the calling to which you have been called, with all lowliness and meekness, with patience, forbearing one another in love, eager to maintain the unity of the Spirit in the bond of peace.

C: **Produce in us the fruit of patience, O Holy Spirit.**

P: The saying is sure and worthy of full acceptance, that Christ Jesus came into the world to save sinners. And I am the foremost of sinners; but I received mercy for this reason, that in me, as the foremost, Jesus Christ might display His perfect patience for an example to those who were to believe in Him for eternal life.

C: **Produce in us the fruit of patience, O Holy Spirit, as our Lord Jesus was patient with us. Amen.**

(Heb. 6:15, 11-12; James 5:7-8; 1 Thess. 5:14-15;
Col. 1:11-12; Eph. 4:1b-3; 1 Tim. 1:15-16)

The Lord's Prayer (All)

The Closing Collect

P: Lord God, heavenly Father, we humbly entreat You for all sorts and conditions of people that You would make known Your ways among us; preserve those who travel; satisfy the wants of Your creatures; help those who call upon You in any need that they may have patience in the midst of suffering and a happy issue out of their afflictions; through Jesus Christ, our Lord.

C: **Amen.**

The Benediction

C: **Amen.**

The Closing Hymn: "Now the Day Is Over"

Acknowledgments

Unless otherwise indicated, Scripture references are from the Revised Standard Version of the Bible, copyrighted 1946, 1952 © 1971, 1973. Used by permission.

Copyright © 1984 Concordia Publishing House

115

Lent 3

Faithfulness from the Passion of Christ

The Silent Prayer

How precious is Your steadfast love, O God! The children of God take refuge in the shadow of Your wings. They feast on the abundance of Your house, and You give them drink from the river of Your delights. For with You is the fountain of life; in Your light do we see light. Amen.

The Hymn of Invocation: "Come to Calvary's Holy Mountain"

The Prayer of Invocation

P: Lord, You have been our dwelling place in all generations. You are from everlasting to everlasting, and Your steadfast love is poured down upon us. In this hour of Lent, we come into Your presence, acknowledging our faithlessness in thought, word, and deed. Our words say one thing; our actions, another. In Your steadfast love and mercy, forgive us. Build our faith, O Lord, that we may faithfully take up the cross and follow You. Enable us to take that first step as we begin in the name of the Father and of the Son and of the Holy Spirit.

C: **Amen.**

The Call to Worship

P: O Lord, I will always sing of Your constant love; I will proclaim Your faithfulness forever.

C: **I know that Your love will last for all time, that Your faithfulness is as permanent as the sky.**

P: You said, "I have made a covenant with the man I chose; I have promised My servant David,

C: **'A descendant of yours will always be king; I will preserve your dynasty forever.'"**

P: The heavens sing of the wonderful things You do; they sing of Your faithfulness, Lord.

C: **No one in heaven is like You, Lord; none of the heavenly beings is Your equal.**

P: You are respected in the council of the holy ones; they all stand in awe of You.

C: Lord God almighty, none is as mighty as You; in all things You are faithful, O Lord.

P: How powerful You are! How great is Your strength!

C: Your kingdom is founded on righteousness and justice; love and faithfulness are shown in all You do.

P: How happy are the people who worship You with songs, who live in the light of Your kindness!

C: Because of You they rejoice all day long, and they praise You for Your goodness.

(Ps. 89:1-8, 13-16 TEV)

The Scripture Reading: Matt. 26:14-16, 20-25, 47-50; 27:1-10

The Sermon Hymn: "O God, My Faithful God"

The Sermon
Text: Matt. 26:47-56

The Offering

The Offertory Hymn: "My Faith Looks Trustingly"

The Litany on Faithfulness

P: I look to the mountains; where will my help come from? My help will come from the Lord, who made heaven and earth.

C: Produce in us the fruit of faithfulness, O Holy Spirit.

P: He will not let you fall; your Protector is always awake.

C: Produce in us the fruit of faithfulness, O Holy Spirit.

P: But if God so clothes the grass which is alive in the field today and tomorrow is thrown into the oven, how much more will He clothe you, O men of little faith?

C: Produce in us the fruit of faithfulness, O Holy Spirit.

P: God is faithful, and He will not let you be tempted beyond your strength, but with the temptation will provide the way of escape, that you may be able to endure it.

C: Produce in us the fruit of faithfulness, O Holy Spirit.

P: The Lord is faithful; He will strengthen you and guard you from evil.

C: Produce in us the fruit of faithfulness, O Holy Spirit.

P: The saying is sure and worthy of full acceptance, that Christ Jesus came into the world to save sinners.

C: Produce in us the fruit of faithfulness, O Holy Spirit.

P: The saying is sure: If we have died with Him, we shall also live with Him; if we endure, we shall also reign with Him.

C: Produce in us the fruit of faithfulness, O Holy Spirit.

P: If we deny Him, He also will deny us; if we are faithless, He remains faithful—for He cannot deny Himself.

C: Produce in us the fruit of faithfulness, O Holy Spirit.

P: Be faithful unto death, and I will give you the crown of life.

C: Produce in us the fruit of faithfulness, O Holy Spirit, as our Lord Jesus was faithful to us.

(Ps. 121:1-3 TEV; Matt. 12:28; 1 Cor. 10:13b;
2 Thess. 3:3; 1 Tim. 1:15; 2 Tim. 2:11-13; Rev. 2:10c)

The Lord's Prayer (All)

The Closing Collect

P: Almighty God, our heavenly Father, out of Your tender love toward us sinners You have given us Your Son that, believing in Him, we might have everlasting life. Continue to grant us Your Holy Spirit that we may remain steadfast in this faith to the end and come to life everlasting; through Jesus Christ, our Lord.

C: Amen.

The Benediction

P: May the God of peace Himself sanctify you wholly, and may your spirit and soul and body be kept sound and blameless at the coming of our Lord Jesus Christ. He who calls you is faithful, and He will do it.

(1 Thess. 5:23-24)

C: Amen.

The Closing Hymn: "All Praise to Thee, My God, This Night"

Acknowledgments

Unless otherwise indicated, Scripture references are from the Revised Standard Version of the Bible, copyrighted 1946, 1952 © 1971, 1973. Used by permission.

Copyright © 1984 Condordia Publishing House

Lent 4

Goodness from the Passion of Christ

The Silent Prayer

O almighty God, from whom every good prayer comes and who pours out on all who desire it the spirit of grace and prayer, deliver us when we draw near to You from coldness of heart and wanderings of mind, that with steadfast thoughts and holy love we may worship You in spirit and in truth, through Jesus Christ, our Lord. Amen.

The Hymn of Invocation: "Jesus, Priceless Treasure"

The Opening Sentences

P: Heavenly Father, we cry to You from the darkness of our lives.

C: Shine through the darkness and grant us Your strength.

P: Lord Jesus, we call to You from the depth of our sins.

C: We know that You are our light and our salvation; therefore, we will not fear, but we will worship You with joy and with love.

P: Holy Spirit, in our weakness we pray for Your help and blessing.

C: Show us Your mercy and help us to reflect Your goodness in our own good words and deeds.

The Confession of Sins

P: Dear friends in Christ, here in the presence of Almighty God, let us with humble and obedient hearts confess our sins so that we may obtain forgiveness by His infinite goodness and mercy.

All: Most merciful God, we confess that we have sinned against You. You have been good to us, and yet we have been slow to thank You by loving our neighbor as ourself. We pray that You will forgive what we have been, amend what we are, and direct what we shall be that we may delight in Your will and walk in Your ways, through Jesus Christ, our Lord. Amen.

P: Almighty God, have mercy on us; forgive us all our sins, through Jesus Christ, our Lord; strengthen us in all goodness, and by the power of the Holy Spirit, keep us in eternal life.

C: Amen.

The Psalm of Forgiveness and Guidance: Ps. 25:1-9 (TEV)

P: To You, O Lord, I offer my prayer; in You, my God, I trust.

C: **Save me from the shame of defeat; don't let my enemies gloat over me!**

P: Defeat does not come to those who trust in You, but to those who are quick to rebel against You.

C: **Teach me Your ways, O Lord; make them known to me. Teach me to live according to your truth, for You are my God, who saves me. I always trust in You.**

P: Remember, O Lord, Your kindness and constant love which You have shown from long ago.

C: **Forgive the sins and errors of my youth. In Your constant love and goodness, remember me, Lord!**

P: Because the Lord is righteous and good, He teaches sinners the path they should follow.

C: **He leads the humble in the right way and teaches them His will.**

All: **Glory be to the Father and to the Son and to the Holy Spirit; as it was in the beginning, is now, and will be forever. Amen.**

The Scripture Reading: John 11:47-50, 53

The Sermon Hymn: "'Come Follow Me,' Said Christ, the Lord"

The Sermon

Text: Matt. 26:57-68

The Offering

The Offertory

All: **Create in me a clean heart, O God, and renew a right spirit within me. Cast me not away from your presence, and take not your Holy Spirit from me. Restore to me the joy of Your salvation, and uphold me with Your free Spirit. Amen.**

The Litany on Goodness

P: What a rich harvest the Lord's goodness provides! Wherever He goes there is plenty. The pastures are filled with flocks; the hillsides are full of joy.

C: **Produce in us the fruit of goodness, O Holy Spirit.**

P: You know about Jesus of Nazareth and how God poured out on Him the Holy Spirit and power. He went everywhere, doing good and healing all who were under the power of the Devil, for God was with Him.

C: **Produce in us the fruit of goodness, O Holy Spirit.**

P: Christ was without sin, but for our sake God made Him share our sin in order that in union with Him we might share the righteousness of God.

C: Produce in us the fruit of goodness, O Holy Spirit.

P: I know that good does not live in me—that is, in my human nature. For even though the desire to do good is in me, I am not able to do it. I don't do the good I want to do.

C: Produce in us the fruit of goodness, O Holy Spirit.

P: We ask our God to make you worthy of the life He has called you to live. May He fulfill by His power all your desire for goodness and complete your work of faith.

C: Produce in us the fruit of goodness, O Holy Spirit.

P: You yourselves used to be in darkness, but since you have become the Lord's people, you are in the light. So you must live like people who belong to the light, for it is the light that brings a rich harvest of every kind of goodness, righteousness, and truth.

C: Produce in us the fruit of goodness, O Holy Spirit.

P: Surely goodness and mercy shall follow me all the days of my life; and I shall dwell in the house of the Lord forever.

C: Produce in us the fruit of goodness, O Holy Spirit.

(Ps 65:12-13 TEV, adapted; Acts 10:38 TEV;
2 Cor. 5:21 TEV; Rom 7:18-19a TEV;
2 Thess. 1:11 TEV; Eph. 5:8-9 TEV; Ps. 23:6)

The Lord's Prayer (All)

The Closing Collect

P: Direct us, O Lord, in all our doings with Your most gracious favor, and further us with Your continual help that in all works begun, continued, and ended in You we may glorify Your holy name and finally by Your mercy obtain eternal salvation; through Jesus Christ, our Lord.

C: Amen.

The Benediction

P: Now may the God of peace...equip you with everything good that you may do His will, working in you that which is pleasing in His sight, through Jesus Christ; to whom be glory forever and ever.

(Heb. 13:20-21)

C: Amen.

The Closing Hymn: "Now Rest Beneath Night's Shadow"

Acknowledgments

Unless otherwise indicated, Scripture references are from the Revised Standard Version of the Bible, copyrighted 1946, 1952 © 1971, 1973. Used by permission.

Copyright © 1984 Concordia Publishing House

121

Lent 5

Self-control from the Passion of Christ

The Hymn of Invocation: "Go to Dark Gethsemane"

The Psalm of Trust: Ps. 63

P: Like a thirsty child reaching for a drink,

C: I grasp for You, O God. And I have found You.

P: I have sensed Your holy presence in the worship service; And in the hour of prayer I have felt You to be near.

C: I realize now that Your love for me is far better than life itself.

P: My heart is full of joy and contentment.

C: My mouth is filled with praises for You.

P: Even the night hours are no longer lonely

C: As I contemplate Your tender concern for me.

P: The enemies of my soul still seek to betray me,

C: But they shall not snatch me out of Your hand.

P: And now that I have found You,

C: I shall be secure and happy forever.

The Prayer of Beginnings

P: We make our beginning in the name of the Triune God:

C: We begin in the name of the Father and of the Son and of the Holy Spirit.

P: We begin in the name of the Father:

C: For in Him the world had its beginning, and each day is begun by His governance.

P: We begin in the name of the Son:

C: For in Him a new age began, a new life was given, and a new hope rose out of death.

P: We begin in the name of the Holy Spirit:

C: For in Him we are called, gathered, enlightened and sanctified.

P: And so we begin, for God is the Lord of new beginnings:

C: **Beginning with us! Thanks be to God: Father, Son, and Holy Spirit! Amen.**

The Scripture Reading: Luke 22:54-62

P: But Thou, O Lord, have mercy upon us!

C: **Thanks be to Thee, O Lord!**

The Sermon Hymn: "In the Hour of Trial"

The Sermon
Text: Matt. 26:69-75

The Offering

The Offertory Hymn: "On My Heart Imprint Your Image"

The Responsive Prayer for Self-control

P: How often, O Lord, our lives are out of control. Temptations stand in our way, and we lose self-control, for, as James says, "each person is tempted when he is lured and enticed by his own desire.

C: **Then desire when it has conceived gives birth to sin; and sin when it is full-grown brings forth death."**

P: Our tongues speak before we think; our tongues speak what we think; our tongues speak what should not be spoken; we lose self-control.

C: **"The tongue is a fire. The tongue is an unrighteous world among our members, staining the whole body, setting on fire the cycle of nature, and set on fire by hell.**

P: For every kind of beast and bird, of reptile and sea creature, can be tamed and has been tamed by humankind.

C: **But no human being can tame the tongue—a restless evil, full of deadly poison.**

P: With it we bless the Lord and Father, and with it we curse men, who are made in the likeness of God.

C: **From the same mouth come blessing and cursing." Lord, give to us the spirit of self-control.**

P: Like Peter, we think we are in control, O lord. We imagine that because we have been Your followers for a good long time, we can stand on our own.

C: **We think that we will not be the ones who will lose our tempers, say the hurting word, do the thoughtless, uncontrolled action.**

P: And then we are out of control. Things, relationships, standards, values, all fall apart.

C: **And we end up in a heap, weeping from inside out, biting our tongues, filled with shame and regret.**

P: Look on us, Lord. Take control. Real control, Lord, the control that King David's out-of-control life pleaded for when he prayed:

C: "Create in me a clean heart, O God, and renew a right spirit within me."

P: Look on us, Lord, Take control.

C: "Cast me not away from Thy presence, and take not Thy holy Spirit from me."

P: Look on us, Lord. Take control, We are not in control. We don't want to be anymore. We don't need to be anymore.

C: Take control, O Lord. Give to us the Spirit's gift of self-control. And then our hearts and minds and tongues and lives will sing in uncontrolled, Spirit-controlled praise to You:

All: "Restore unto me the joy of Thy salvation; and uphold me with Thy free Spirit." Amen.

The Lord's Prayer (All)

The Closing Collect

P: Almighty, everlasting God, whose Son has assured forgiveness of sins and deliverance from eternal death, strengthen us by Your Holy Spirit that our faith in Christ increase daily and we hold fast the hope that we shall not die but fall asleep and on the last day be raised to eternal life; through Jesus Christ, our Lord.

C: Amen.

The Benediction

C: Amen.

The Closing Hymn: "O Trinity, O Blessed Light"

Acknowledgments

Ps. 63 from *Good Lord, Where Are You?* © 1967 by CPH. Closing Collect from *Lutheran Worship*, © 1982 by CPH.

Copyright © 1984 Concordia Publishing House

Lent 6

Peace from the Passion of Christ

The Silent Prayer

Most holy God, the Source of all good desires, all right judgments, and all just works: Give to us, Your servants, that peace which the world cannot give so that our minds may be fixed on the doing of Your will, and that we, being delivered from the fear of enemies, may live in peace and quietness, through the mercies of Christ Jesus, our Savior. Amen.

The Hymn of Invocation: "Holy Spirit, Light Divine"

The Invocation

P: Grace and peace be to you from God our Father and the Lord Jesus Christ.

C: May His grace and peace be with you also as we worship our Lord together.

The Prayer of Confession

All: Lord God, You know how prone our hearts are to strife, mistrust and temper: come to us and help us, and grant peace in our lives. Forgive us for praying so little, for our lack of love, for stubbornly insisting upon our rights, and make us to know that without Your peace our hearts will have no peace. Give us, O God, the will to be reconciled to You and thus to one another, through Jesus Christ our Lord. Amen.

The Promise of God

P: Our great God does promise forgiveness, peace, and new life to us because of what Jesus Christ has done as our Savior. "I know the plans I have for you," says the Lord, "plans for welfare and not for evil, to give you a future and a hope. Then You will call upon Me and come and pray to Me, and I will hear you."

(Jer. 29:11-12)

C: O God, You will keep those in perfect peace whose mind is steadfast in You, for in returning and rest we shall be saved; in quietness and trust shall be our strength.

The Prayer for Help: Ps. 4 (TEV)

P: Answer me when I pray, O God, my Defender! When I was in trouble, You

125

helped me. Be kind to me now and hear my prayer.

C: **How long will you people insult me? How long will you love what is worthless and go after what is false?**

P: Remember that the Lord has chosen the righteous for His own, and He hears me when I call to Him.

C: **Tremble with fear and stop sinning; think deeply about this, when you lie in silence on your beds.**

P: Offer the right sacrifices to the Lord, and put your trust in Him.

C: **There are many who pray: "Give us more blessings, O Lord. Look on us with kindness!"**

P: But the joy that You have given me is more than they will ever have with all their grain and wine.

C: **When I lie down, I go to sleep in peace; You alone, O Lord, keep me perfectly safe.**

The Scripture Reading: John 18:28-19:16; Luke 19:41-44

The Sermon Hymn: "Glory Be to Jesus"

The Sermon
Text: Matt. 27:11-24

The Greeting of Peace

All: **Heavenly Father, look from heaven upon all Your people and upon this congregation. Give us Your peace, Your love, and Your help. Send us the gifts of Your Spirit so that with a clean heart and a good conscience we may greet one another, not deceitfully nor hypocritically, but purely, in the bond of peace and love. Take from us the desire to control the freedom of others, for there is only one body and one Spirit and one faith into which we have all been called. Bring us to the fullness of Your love in Jesus Christ, our Lord, with whom You are blessed in the unity of the Spirit, one God, forever and ever. Amen.**

P: The peace of the Lord be with you always.

C: **And also with you.**

(All present may now greet one another with the words: "Peace be with you.")

The Offering

The Offertory Hymn: "Alas! And Did My Savior Bleed"

The Litany on Peace

P: Jesus came closer to the city, and when He saw it, He wept over it, saying, "If you only knew today what is needed for peace."

C: **When people say, "There is peace and security," then sudden destruction**

126

will come upon them as travail comes upon a woman with child, and there will be no escape.

P: Jesus told His disciples, "I have said this to you, that in Me you may have peace. In the world you have tribulation, but be of good cheer, I have overcome the world.

C: **Peace is what I leave with you; it is My own peace that I give you. I do not give it as the world does. Do not be worried or upset; do not be afraid."**

P: For Christ is our peace, who has made us both one, and has broken down the dividing wall of hostility. And He came and preached peace to you who were far off and peace to those who were near; for through Him we both have access in one Spirit to the Father.

C: **Therefore, since we are justified by faith, we have peace with God through our Lord Jesus Christ. Through Him we have obtained access to this grace in which we stand, and we rejoice in our hope of sharing the glory of God.**

P: For the kingdom of God does not mean food and drink but righteousness and peace and joy in the Holy Spirit.

C: **Let us then pursue what makes for peace and for mutual upbuilding.**

P: Mend your ways, heed my appeal, agree with one another, live in peace, and the God of love and peace will be with you.

C: **And may the peace of Christ rule in our hearts, to which indeed we were called in the one body.**

P: To be controlled by human nature results in death; to be controlled by the Spirit results in life and peace.

All: **Lord, now lettest Thou Thy servant depart in peace according to Thy word; for mine eyes have seen Thy salvation.**

(Luke 19: 41-42 TEV; 1 Thess. 5:3; John 16:33 adapted; 14:27 TEV; Eph. 2:14, 17; Rom 5:1-2; 14:17, 19; Col. 3:15; Rom. 8:6 TEV; Matt. 2:29-30 adapted)

The Lord's Prayer (All)

The Closing Collect

P: O God, from whom all holy desires, all good counsels, and all just works proceed, give to your servants that peace which the world cannot give that our hearts may be set to obey your commandments and also that we, being defended by you, may pass our time in rest and quietness; through the merits of Jesus Christ, our Savior.

C: **Amen.**

The Benediction

P: Now may the Lord of peace Himself give you peace at all times in all ways. The Lord be with you all.

C: Amen.

The Closing Hymn: "On My Heart Imprint Your Image"

Acknowledgments

Unless otherwise indicated, Scripture references are from the Revised Standard Version of the Bible, copyrighted 1946, 1952 © 1971, 1973. Used by permission.

Closing collect from *Lutheran Worship*, © 1982, CPH.

Copyright © 1984 Concordia Publishing House

Kindness from the Passion of Christ

The Hymn of Invocation: "A Lamb Alone Bears Willingly"

The Call to Worship

P: Jesus said, "I did not come to invite virtuous people, but sinners."
Merciful God, we do not dare to come to this table trusting in our own
goodness and virtue. We come because we are sinful people and need
forgiveness. We come because we are hungry for life and need to be fed.

C: Father, forgive us and feed us.

P: We come because Christ has invited us sinners. We come in gratitude and
wonder to offer our very selves to You in worship and adoration.

C: Father, accept our paise;

All: Through Jesus Christ, our Lord.

The Responsive Reading of the Passover Account

P: The Lord spoke to Moses and Aaron in Egypt:

C: "This month is to be the first month of the year for you.

P: Give these instructions to the whole community of Israel: On the 10th day
of this month each man must choose either a lamb or a young goat for
his household.

**C: If his family is too small to eat a whole animal, he and his next-door
neighbor may share an animal, in proportion to the number of people and
the amount that each person can eat.**

P: You may choose either a sheep or a goat, but it must be a one-year-old
male without any defects.

**C: Then, on the evening of the 14th day of the month, the whole community
of Israel will kill the animals.**

P: The people are to take some of the blood and put it on the doorposts and
above the doors of the houses in which the animals are to be eaten.

**C: That night the meat is to be roasted and eaten with bitter herbs and with
bread made without yeast.**

P: Do not eat any of it raw or boiled, but eat it roasted whole, including the head, the legs, and the internal organs.

C: **You must not leave any of it until morning; if any is left over, it must be burned.**

P: You are to eat it quickly, for you are to be dressed for travel, with your sandals on your feet and your walking stick in your hand. It is the Passover Festival to honor Me, the Lord.

C: **On that night I will go through the land of Egypt, killing every firstborn male, both human and animal, and punishing all the gods of Egypt. I am the Lord.**

P: The blood on the doorposts will be a sign to mark the houses in which you live. When I see the blood, I will pass over you and will not harm you when I punish the Egyptians.

C: **You must celebrate this day as a religious festival to remind you of what I, the Lord, have done. Celebrate it for all time to come."**

(Ex. 12:2-14 TEV)

The Epistle: 1 Cor. 11:23-29

The Holy Gospel: Luke 22:7-20

The Sermon Hymn: "Lord Jesus Christ, You Have Prepared"

The Maundy Thursday Message

Text: Matt. 26:26-29

The Offering

The Offertory Hymn: "Do Not Despair, O Little Flock"

The Litany on Kindness

All: **"Thou art a God ready to pardon, gracious and merciful, slow to anger, and of great kindness."**

P: O Lord, on that Maundy Thursday evening when You were so weighted down with the events that were destined from eternity to occur, You still cared for Your own followers and showed them kindness.

C: **Give to us the Spirit's fruit of kindness, O Lord.**

P: You took the towel and the basin. You stooped down to wash the disciples' feet.

C: **Give to us the Spirit's fruit of kindness, O Lord.**

P: Although death was at hand, You pointed beyond death and showed the mansions in our Father's House.

C: **Give to us the Spirit's fruit of kindness, O Lord.**

P: Although hatred would soon have its way for a time, You pointed to the great command: "Love one another even as I have loved you."

C: **Give to us the Spirit's fruit of kindness, O Lord.**

P: Although Your friends would this night abandon You and flee, You promised them: "It is to your advantage that I go away, for if I do not go away, the Counselor will not come to you; but if I go, I will send Him to you."

C: **Give to us the Spirit's fruit of kindness, O Lord.**

P: Although Your friends this night would not even stay awake to pray, You prayed the great High Priestly Prayer for them and for us.

C: **Give to us the Spirit's fruit of kindness, O Lord.**

P: And then, in the deepest kindness of all, You broke the bread and shared the cup. You gave them, You give us, Yourself, Your true body and blood.

C: **Give to us the Spirit's fruit of kindness, O Lord.**

All: **"Let us rend our hearts and not our garments and turn unto the Lord our God; for He is gracious and merciful, slow to anger, and of great kindness." Amen.**

(Neh. 9:17b KJV; John 13:34; 16:7b; Joel 2:13 KJV)

The Confession and Absolution

P: I confess to God Almighty, before the whole company of heaven and to you, my brothers and sisters, that I have sinned in thought, word, and deed by my fault, by my own fault, by my own most grievous fault; wherefore I pray God Almighty to have mercy on me, forgive me all my sins, and bring me to everlasting life. Amen.

C: **The almighty and merciful Lord grant you pardon, forgiveness, and remission of all your sins. Amen.**

C: **I confess to God almighty, before the whole company of heaven and to you, my brothers and sisters, that I have sinned in thought, word, and deed by my fault, by my own fault, by my own most grievous fault; wherefore I pray God Almighty to have mercy on me, forgive me all my sins, and bring me to everlasting life. Amen.**

P: The almighty and merciful Lord grant you pardon, forgiveness, and remission of all your sins.

The Lord's Prayer (All)

The Consecration

P: The Lord be with you.

C: **And with your spirit.**

P: Lift up your hearts.

C: **We lift them to the Lord.**

P: Let us give thanks to the Lord, our God.

C: **It is right to do so.**

131

P: On the night He was betrayed—

C: **He came to be like us that we might be more like Him.**

P: He took bread—

C: **He came to share our life that we might know what true sharing and breaking is to be in our lives.**

P: And when He had given thanks—

C: **We come to see the real Christ in the Supper: His forgetfulness of self against our self-centeredness; His humility against our foolish pride; His trust against our doubts and fears.**

P: He broke it and gave it—

C: **"God so loved the world that He gave His only-begotten Son...."**

P: He gave it to His disciples—

C: **"Truly, I say to you, unless you turn and become like little children, you will never enter the kingdom of heaven."**

P: Saying, Take! Eat!—

C: **Take forgiveness, love, and the very miracle of Christ Himself. Take it as a gift offered.**

P: This is My   body—

C: **"And Joseph took the body and wrapped it in a clean linen shroud and laid it in his own new tomb."**

P: My body, which is given for you—

C: **"Whatever you ask in My name, I will do it...."**

P: Do this to remember Me—

C: **"I will not leave you desolate; I will come to you. Yet a little while, and the world will see Me no more. But you will see Me; because I live, you will live also."**

P: After the same manner also He took the cup—

C: **"The cup that I drink, you will drink, and with the baptism with which I am baptized, you will be baptized."**

P: And when He had had His supper and had given thanks, He gave it to them, saying, Drink it, all of you! This is My   blood—

C: **"Then I saw a new heaven and a new earth....and I saw the holy city, new Jerusalem...and I heard a loud voice from the throne, saying, "Behold, the dwelling of God is with men. He will dwell with them, and they shall be His people, and God Himself will be with them....Behold, I make all things new!"**

P: Shed for you and for many—

C: "Judge not, that you be not judged." For God is love, and His love acts to set people free.

P: For the forgiveness of sins—

C: "For the wages of sin is death, but the free gift of God is eternal life in Christ Jesus, our Lord."

P: Do this as often as you drink it, remembering Me.

C: May it ever be so. Amen! Amen!

P: Come to the Lord's Table!

(Based on Matt. 26:26-28; John 3:16a KJV;
Matt. 18:3; 27:59-60a; John 14:13, 18-19;
Mark 10:39; Rev. 21:1-5a; Matt. 7:1; Rom 6:23)

The Distribution of the Holy Communion

The Thanksgiving

P: As often as you eat this bread and drink this cup:

C: You do show the Lord's death until He comes!

The Closing Collect

P: Dear Lord Jesus, we thank and praise You that You have again refreshed us with the gift of Your holy body and blood in this comforting sacrament. Bless our participation that we may depart from Your presence with peace and joy in the knowledge that we are reconciled to God. We ask this in Your name.

C: Amen.

P: The Lord be with you.

C: And with your spirit.

P: Bless we the Lord.

C: Thanks be to God.

The Benediction

C: Amen.

The Closing Hymn: "O Living Bread from Heaven"

Acknowledgments

Unless otherwise indicated, Scripture references are from the Revised Standard Version of the Bible, copyrighted 1946, 1952 © 1971, 1973. Used by permission.

The preface dialog is from the International Consultation on English Texts.

Copyright © 1984 Concordia Publishing House

Good Friday

Love from the Passion of Christ

The Hymn of Invocation: "When I Survey the Wondrous Cross"

The Opening Litany on Love

P: I have loved you with an everlasting love; therefore I have continued my faithfulness to you.

C: This is what love is: it is not that we have loved God, but that He loved us and sent His Son to be the means by which our sins are forgiven.

P: You shall love the Lord your God with all your heart, and with all your soul, and with all your mind.

C: This is what love is: it is not that we have loved God, but that He loved us and sent His Son to be the means by which our sins are forgiven.

P: You shall love your neighbor as yourself.

C: This is what love is: it is not that we have loved God, but that He loved us and sent His Son to be the means by which our sins are forgiven.

P: Love your enemies; do good to those who hate you; bless those who curse you; pray for those who abuse you.

C: This is what love is: it is not that we have loved God, but that He loved us and sent His Son to be the means by which our sins are forgiven.

P: And this is the judgment, that the light has come into the world, and men loved the darkness rather than light, because their deeds were evil.

C: This is what love is: it is not that we have loved God, but that He loved us and sent His Son to be the means by which our sins are forgiven.

P: But God shows His love for us in that while we were yet sinners Christ died for us.

C: This is what love is: it is not that we have loved God, but that He loved us and sent His Son to be the means by which our sins are forgiven.

P: Greater love has no man than this, that [he] lay down his life for his friends.

C: This is what love is: it is not that we have loved God, but that He loved us and sent His Son to be the means by which our sins are forgiven.

All: For God so loved the world that He gave His only-begotten Son, that

134

whosoever believeth in Him should not perish but have everlasting life. Amen.

(Jer. 31:3b; 1 John 4:10 TEV; Matt. 22:37, 39b; Luke 6:27b-28; John 3:19; Rom. 5:8; John 15:13; John 3:16 KJV)

The Hymn: "Jesus, Your Boundless Love So True"

The Epistle: Heb. 4:14-16; 5:7-9

The Holy Gospel: John 19:17-30

The Sermon Hymn: "Jesus, in Your Dying Woes"

The Sermon

    Text: Mark 15:33-39

The Offering

The Offertory Hymn: "Love Divine, All Love Excelling"

The Good Friday Responsive Reading on Love

P: If I speak in the tongues of men and of angels, but have not love:

C: I am a noisy gong or a clanging cymbal.

P: And if I have prophetic powers, and understand all mysteries and all knowledge, and if I have all faith, so as to remove mountains, but have not love:

C: I am nothing.

P: If I give away all I have, and if I deliver my body to be burned, but have not love:

C: I gain nothing.

P: Love is patient and kind; love is not jealous or boastful; it is not arrogant or rude.

C: Love does not insist on its own way; it is not irritable or resentful;

P: It does not rejoice at wrong, but rejoices in the right.

C: Love bears all things, believes all things, hopes all things, endures all things.

P: Love never ends; as for prophecies, they will pass away; as for tongues, they will cease; as for knowledge, it will pass away.

C: For our knowledge is imperfect and our prophecy is imperfect; but when the perfect comes, the imperfect will pass away.

P: When I was a child, I spoke like a child, I thought like a child, I reasoned like a child; when I became a man, I gave up childish ways.

C: For now we see in a mirror dimly, but then face to face.

P: Now I know in part; then I shall understand fully,

C: Even as I have been fully understood.

P: So faith, hope, love abide, these three;

C: **But the greatest of these is love.**

P: Beloved, let us love one another; for love is of God.

C: **And he who loves is born of God and knows God.**

P: He who does not love does not know God;

C: **For God is love.**

P: In this the love of God was made manifest among us,

C: **That God sent His only Son into the world, so that we might live through Him.**

P: In this is love, not that we loved God but that He loved us and sent His Son

C: **To be the expiation for our sins.**

All: **For God so loved the world that He gave His only-begotten Son, that whosoever believeth in Him should not perish but have everlasting life.**

(1 Cor. 13; 1 John 4:7-10; John 3:16 KJV)

The Hymn: "O Sacred Head, Now Wounded"

The Good Friday Litany

P: O Lord, have mercy upon us.

C: **O Lord, have mercy upon us.**

P: O Christ, have mercy upon us.

C: **O Christ, have mercy upon us.**

P: O Lord, have mercy upon us.

C: **O Lord, have mercy upon us.**

P: O Christ, hear Thou us.

C: **O Christ, hear Thou us.**

P: O God, the Father in heaven,

C: **Have mercy upon us.**

P: O God, the Holy Spirit,

C: **Have mercy upon us.**

P: Be gracious unto us.

C: **Spare us, good Lord.**

P: O Lord, Jesus Christ, Son of God,

C: **We beseech You to hear us.**

P: O Lamb of God, that takest away the sin of the world,

C: **Have mercy upon us.**

P: O Lamb of God, that takest away the sin of the world,

C: Grant us Your peace.

P: O Christ, hear Thou us.

C: O Christ, hear Thou us.

P: O Lord, have mercy upon us.

C: O Lord, have mercy upon us.

P: O Christ, have mercy upon us.

C: O Christ, have mercy upon us.

The Lord's Prayer (All)

The Benediction

C: Amen.

Acknowledgments

Unless otherwise indicated, Scripture references are from the Revised Standard Version of the Bible, copyrighted 1946, 1952 © 1971, 1973. Used by permission.

Copyright © 1984 Concordia Publishing House

Joy from the Passion of Christ

(The followers of Jesus on that first Easter morning came to the tomb fully expecting nothing more than the opportunity to prepare Jesus' body for the sleep of death. His burial on Good Friday had been done in haste; now they would take more time for a proper preparation of their beloved Master's body. On this Easter morning, we signal this same mood with the bare chancel, the somber confession, and the sorrowful hymn of death.)

The Pre-Easter Reading: John 19:38-42; Mark 16:1-3

Our Journey to the Tomb: A Time of Confession

P: Lord God, our heavenly Father, we walk in spirit with those who went to the tomb early Easter morning.

C: **And we walk with all the mourners everywhere who have suffered and who are still suffering. Color the world this morning dark and gray and sad.**

P: For if Christ has not been raised, our faith is futile and we are still in our sins.

C: **Our words of confession would bounce back to accuse us. Our sins of thought and word and deed would stamp us guilty. We would continue to exist in the death called sin.**

P: The sealed tomb seals our fate. Then even God Himself cannot rescue us from what we are.

C: **The world would go on toward death, sealed with the curse of the Fall, with pain and suffering and cruelty and meaningless life and death for all.**

P: If Christ has not been raised, then those who die have perished forever.

C: **The grave would have won, for if one like Christ cannot conquer, how can we?**

P: So we come to the tomb this morning, with only one thing in mind:

C: **To better prepare His body for the sleep of death, and to prepare ourselves for the same sorry sleep. For if Christ has not been raised, we are the most pitiful of people.**

All: **But who will roll away the stone—Pilate's stone, the stone of death, the stone of sin that blocks the way to God?**

The Hymn: "Go to Dark Gethsemane"

(The congregation shall stand.)

The Easter Gospel: Mark 16:1-8

Our Journey to the Tomb: A Time of Resurrection

P: People of God, why do you seek the living among the dead?

C: Because we have nowhere else to go. He had told us that He is the Way, the Truth, and the Life.

P: People of God, why do you seek the living among the dead?

C: Because we live in a world that still suffers from wars and hunger, cruelty and bloodshed. Because families are torn apart by greed or death or selfishness. Because individual lives deny or ignore or mock God.

P: People of God, approach the tomb! Await the dawn of a new age! Seek the miracle of new life! People of God, why do you seek the living among the dead?

C: Because we remember His words of resurrection and life and hope and victory.

P: People of God, do not live in death. Do not let sin be your master. Jesus Christ has risen to forgive you. He has risen to save you. He has risen to give you life. People of God, He is not here. He is risen!

C: Yes, the tomb is empty. He is risen!

P: He is risen!

C: And He is among us!

P: Alleluia!

C: Alleluia!

P: He is risen!

C: He is risen indeed!

The Processional

(During the Processional the Easter flowers will be brought forward and placed in the chancel, the Easter banner will be displayed, and the altar cross will be unveiled.)

The Hymn of Resurrection: "Jesus Christ Is Risen Today"

The Introit

All: Alleluia. [Christ] has risen, as he said.*
He has risen from the dead. Alleluia.
Give thanks to the Lord, for he is good;*
his love endures forever.

Let Israel say:*
    "His love endures forever."
I was pushed back and about to fall,*
    but the Lord helped me.
I will give you thanks, for you answered me;*
    you have become my salvation.
The stones the builders rejected*
    has become the capstone:
This is the day the Lord has made*
    let us rejoice and be glad in it.
Blessed is he who comes in the name of the Lord,*
    from the house of the Lord we bless you.
Glory be to the Father and to the Son*
    and to the Holy Spirit;
as it was in the beginning,*
    is now, and will be forever. Amen.
Alleluia. [Christ] has risen, as he said.*
    He has risen from the dead. Alleluia.

The Kyrie

P: In peace let us pray to the Lord.

C: **Lord, have mercy.**

P: For the peace from above and for our salvation, let us pray to the Lord.

C: **Lord, have mercy.**

P: For the peace of the whole world, for the well-being of the Church of God, and for the unity of all, let us pray to the Lord.

C: **Lord, have mercy.**

P: For this holy house, and for all who offer here their worship and praise, let us pray to the Lord.

C: **Lord, have mercy.**

P: Help, save, comfort, and defend us, gracious Lord.

C: **Amen.**

The Hymn of Praise

All: **This is the feast of victory for our God. Alleluia, alleluia, alleluia.**

    Worthy is Christ, the Lamb who was slain, whose blood set us free to be people of God. This is the feast of victory for our God. Alleluia, alleluia, alleluia.

    Power, riches, widsom, and strength, and honor, blessing, and glory are his. This is the feast of victory for our God. Alleluia, alleluia, alleluia.

    Sing with all the people of God, and join in the hymn of all creation:

Blessing, honor, glory, and might be to God and the Lamb forever. Amen. This is the feast of victory for our God. Alleluia, alleluia, alleluia.

For the Lamb who was slain has begun his reign. Alleluia. This is the feast of victory for our God. Alleluia, alleluia, alleluia.

The Collect of the Day

P: The Lord be with you.

C: And also with you.

P: Let us pray. Almighty God the Father, through Your only-begotten Son Jesus Christ You have overcome death and opened the gate of everlasting life to us. Grant that we, who celebrate with joy the day of our Lord's resurrection, may be raised from the death of sin by Your life-giving Spirit; through Jesus Christ, our Lord, who lives and reigns with You and the Holy Spirit, one God, now and forever.

C: Amen.

The Easter Epistle: 1 Cor. 15:19-28

The Sermon Hymn: "I Know That My Redeemer Lives"

The Sermon
Text: John 20:11-18

The Offering

The Offertory

All: Let the vineyards be fruitful, Lord, and fill to the brim our cup of blessing. Gather a harvest from the seeds that were sown that we may feed with the bread of life. Gather the hopes and dreams of all; unite them with the prayers we offer now. Grace our table with your presence, and give us a foretaste of the feast to come.

The Responsive Easter Prayer of Joy in the Lord.

P: "When the Lord restored the fortunes of Zion, we were like those who dream.

C: Then our mouth was filled with laughter, and our tongue with shouts of joy;

P: Then they said among the nations, 'The Lord has done great things for them.'

C: The Lord has done great things for us; we are glad.

P: Restore our fortunes, O Lord, like the watercourses in the Negeb!

C: May those who sow in tears reap with shouts of joy!

P: He that goes forth weeping, bearing the seed for sowing,

C: Shall come home with shouts of joy, bringing his sheaves with him."

P: On this happy Day of Resurrection, give to us joy, O Lord, that we may "rejoice before Thee as with joy at the harvest..."

C: **Or as people who return from bondage who "Come to Zion with singing; everlasting joy shall be upon their heads; they shall obtain joy and gladness, and sorrow and sighing shall flee away."**

P: Give to us joy, O Lord, joy like that of finding a "treasure hidden in a field, which a man found and covered up; then in his joy he goes and sells all that he has and buys that field;"

C: **Or the joy of finding the lost sheep, the "joy in heaven over one sinner who repents...."**

P: Give to us joy, O Lord, that we may look to "Jesus the Pioneer and Perfecter of our faith, who for the joy that was set before Him endured the cross, despising the shame, and is seated at the right hand of the throne of God."

C: **Give us that joy, O Risen Lord!**

P: Give to us the joy of Peter and John, who saw and believed that Jesus was truly risen from the dead;

C: **And the joy of Mary Magdalene, whose tears of sorrow were turned to tears of joy at the sound of her name from the Master's lips.**

P: Give to us joy, Lord, all the days of our life—the joy of forgiveness, life, and salvation;

C: **And the Spirit's gifts of love, joy, peace, patience, kindness, goodness, faithfulness, gentleness, self-control;**

All: **The gift of the risen Lord Jesus Christ, Conqueror of sin and death, Savior, Lord of all, who gives us all joy forever and ever. Amen.**

(Ps. 126; Is. 9:3b; 51:11; Matt. 13:44;
Luke 15:7; Heb. 12:2)

The Holy Communion

P: The Lord be with you.

C: **And also with you.**

P: Lift up your hearts.

C: **We lift them to the Lord.**

P: Let us give thanks to the Lord our God.

C: **It is right to give Him thanks and praise.**

P: It is truly good, right, and salutary that we should at all times and in all places give thanks to you, holy Lord, almighty Father, everlasting God; but chiefly are we bound to praise you for the glorious resurrection of your Son, Jesus Christ, our Lord; for he is the very Paschal Lamb, which was offered for us and has taken away the sins of the world. By his death he has destroyed death, and by his rising to life again he has restored to us

142

everlasting life. Therefore with angels and archangels and with all the company of heaven we laud and magnify your glorious name, evermore praising you and saying:

C: **Holy, holy, holy Lord, God of pow'r and might: Heaven and earth are full of your glory. Hosanna. Hosanna. Hosanna in the highest. Blessed is he who comes in the name of the Lord. Hosanna in the highest.**

P: Blessed are you, Lord of heaven and earth, for you have had mercy on us children of men and given your only-begotten Son that whoever believes in him should not perish but have eternal life. We give you thanks for the redemption you have prepared for us through Jesus Christ. Send your Holy Spirit into our hearts that he may establish in us a living faith and prepare us joyfully to remember our Redeemer and receive him who comes to us in his body and blood.

C: **Amen.**

The Lord's Prayer (All)

The Words of Institution

The Agnus Dei

All: **Lamb of God, you take away the sin of the world; have mercy on us. Lamb of God, you take away the sin of the world; have mercy on us. Lamb of God, you take away the sin of the world; grant us peace.**

The Distribution

The Distribution Hymns
"O Sons and Daughters of the King"
"Christ the Lord Is Risen Today"
"Awake, My Heart, with Gladness"

The Post-Communion Canticle

All: **Thank the Lord and sing His praise; tell ev'ryone what He has done. Let all who seek the Lord rejoice and proudly bear His name. He recalls His promises and leads His people forth in joy with shouts of thanksgiving. Alleluia. Alleluia.**

The Closing Prayer

P: Let us pray. We give thanks to you, almighty God, that you have refreshed us through this salutary gift, and we implore you that of your mercy you would strengthen us through the same in faith toward you and in fervent love toward one another; through Jesus Christ, your Son, our Lord, who lives and reigns with you and the Holy Spirit, one God, now and forever.

C: **Amen.**

The Benediction

  C: Amen.

The Recessional Hymn: "Jesus Lives, the Victory's Won"

Acknowledgments

The introit, collect of the day, Easter preface, Communion prayer, Agnus Dei, and closing prayer are from *Lutheran Worship*, © 1982, CPH.

The Kyrie, "Worthy is Christ," "Let the vineyards be fruitful," and post-Communion canticle are from *Lutheran Book of Worship*, © 1978, CPH representing the publishers and copyright holders. Used by permission.

The preface dialog and "Holy, holy, holy Lord" are from the International Consultation on English texts.

Unless otherwise indicated, Scripture references are from the Revised Standard Version of the Bible, copyrighted 1946, 1952 © 1971, 1973. Used by permission.

Copyright © 1984 Concordia Publishing House